LIBRARY OF AMERICAN
INDIAN HISTORY

REAPING THE WHIRLWIND

The Apache Wars

Peter Aleshire

Facts On File, Inc.

TO ELISSA AND SETH, CALEB AND NOAH

▲

Reaping the Whirlwind: The Apache Wars

Facts On File, Inc.
11 Penn Plaza
New York NY 10001

Library of Congress Cataloging-in-Publication Data

Aleshire, Peter.
    Reaping the whirlwind : the Apache wars / Peter Aleshire.
        p.   cm.—(Library of American Indian history)
    Includes bibliographical references and index.
    Summary: Examines the question of why policy makers and leaders on both sides of the Apache conflict sowed winds of injustice, hatred, and violence throughout the Southwest for three decades.
    ISBN 0-8160-3602-0
    1. Apache Indians—Wars, 1872–1873—Juvenile literature.
    2. Apache Indians—Wars, 1883–1886—Juvenile Literature.   3. Apache Indians—Government relations—Juvenile literature. [1. Apache Indians—Wars. 2. Indians of North America—Southwest, New.]
    I. Title. II. Series.
    E99.A6A58 1998
    973.8—dc21   97-22772

Facts On File books are available at special discounts when purchased in bulk quantities for businesses, associations, institutions or sales promotions. Please call our Special Sales Department in New York at (212) 967-8800 or (800) 322-8755.

You can find Facts On File on the World Wide Web at http://www.factsonfile.com

Text design by Robert Yaffe
Series cover design byAmy Beth Gonzalez
Cover design by Sholto Ainslie
Illustrations on pages 11, 51, 124 by Jeremy Eagle

Printed in the United States of America

MP FOF 10 9 8 7 6 5 4 3 2 1

This book is printed on acid-free paper.

CONTENTS

▲

AUTHOR'S NOTE

Writing an accurate and compelling history of the Apache wars presents several problems, especially when describing historical accounts to a modern audience used to the way in which TV cameras, videotape, reporters with notebooks, and modern cameras record historical detail. Photographers and reporters almost never accompanied the cavalry units in the field during the Apache wars. That means we must rely heavily on official army reports, which often proved inaccurate, incomplete, or self-serving, augmented by the first-person recollections of people involved. However, most of those firsthand memoirs were written years after the events described, which introduces additional problems.

The problem of reconstruction grows even worse when it comes to detailing the Apache point of view, since they had no written language when first encountered by whites. Few of the primary participants on the Apache side left their own firsthand accounts. The few, contemporary firsthand Apache accounts were filtered through interpreters working for the army—which often meant multiple translations involving Apache, Spanish, and English. Moreover, the accuracy of the interpretation was sometimes a critical issue and often caused conflicts. Fortunately, anthropologist Frank Goodwin and historian Eve Ball some years after these events gathered first-person accounts and oral traditions from

Apache survivors. Those accounts, often translated into English decades after the events in question, sometimes provided sharply different versions of events.

Now, historians and readers must sort through these conflicting accounts, and keep in mind the limitations of the primary sources—especially when it comes to the use of direct quotes and the contrast between American and Apache versions of events. In this account, all of the dialogue used was reported in various primary accounts by people who were present. However, that doesn't mean the dialogue is as accurate as it would be if someone present was taking down the conversations as they happened. Often, the participants put the dialogue into their accounts written many years after the actual events. These quotes may be accurate in spirit, but still are not verbatim quotes as you might find in a modern account by a professional reporter. Only during some of the peace negotiations was someone carefully recording what was said—and even then modern readers must account for the confounding effect of multiple translations from Apache, to Spanish, and finally to English.

INTRODUCTION

▲

A LETHAL PUZZLE

*They have sown the wind, and they shall
reap the whirlwind*

—Hosea 8: 7

Here is a puzzle. In the late 1800s, several thousand Apache who could not make bullets faced several million Americans backed by an advanced industrial culture. The Apache didn't have a chance. The Americans knew it from the start. The Apache came to know it, long before the end. The last of the free Apache warriors quit calling themselves "The People" and started calling themselves *Indeh*—"the Dead." Their name for the whites was *Indah*—"The Living."

Most of the Apache leaders advocated peace. Most soon showed themselves willing to stop raiding, settle on reservations, and live on hunting and rations. They generally tried to keep their warriors in check, accepted the loss of most of their homeland, and even helped the U.S. Army hunt down their own relatives who refused to settle on the reservation. The Americans who led the 40-year war against the Apache generally agreed that the help of the Apache scouts who turned against the renegades was crucial in almost every military success.

This photo, the first taken of Geronimo, by Frank Randall in 1884, remains one of the most famous portraits of an American Indian. *(Courtesy Arizona Historical Society, Tucson, Photo AHS 19501)*

On the American side, many people sympathized with the Apache and supported settling the Indians on reservations and providing them with rations and supplies. The abolitionists who pushed for the elimination of slavery also took up the cause of the

Indian. Many of the leading officers who wrote about the Apache wars heaped praise on their Indian adversaries and penned scathing criticisms of corrupt contractors, murderous whites, and scheming government officials. The Americans also adhered to a religion that advocated charity, mercy, love, honesty, and brotherhood.

So here's the puzzle: Why did the war continue? Why did the war-makers always win out over the peacemakers? Why did the warfare between the Americans and the Apache spring so quickly from the initially peaceful contacts in the late 1840s, and why did it continue so relentlessly until 1886 when a handful of warriors with Geronimo finally surrendered? What forces of history, culture, economics, and myth on both sides propelled the conflict to its needless, brutal, but seemingly inevitable conclusion? Why did the policy makers and leaders on both sides repeatedly sow the winds of injustice, hatred, and violence and so reap the whirlwind of death that convulsed the Southwest for three decades?

That's the question posed by this slender account of those fascinating events. Answering it explains a lot about American history and the roots of all warfare. The haunting history of that war shows that people must live with their contradictions and their choices—and so become what their choices make them.

SETTING THE STAGE FOR TRAGEDY

1400s–1860

Looking back, the conflict between the warrior culture of the Apache and the greedy, expansionist culture of the Americans has an air of inevitability. The independent, free-ranging Apache bands were well adapted to warfare, which enabled them to offer longer, more determined resistance to the spread of European-based civilization than any other Indian culture. They came to the Southwest relatively late in historical terms. Descended from other Athapascan-speaking groups whose homeland was deep in the wilds of Canada and Alaska, the Apache are linguistically related to the Navajo. They migrated south out of Canada as early as A.D. 850 and later became known as Apache—probably as a result of the Spanish adoption of the Zuni term for them, which means "enemy." The scattered Apache bands relied mostly on hunting and gathering, and raids on pueblo peoples, the Navajo, and each other. Evidence suggests the Apache did not become heavily dependent on raiding until after the arrival of the Spanish in the 1600s. The Apache lived in related family bands scattered throughout the mountain ranges of Arizona, New Mexico, and northern Mexico. These family bands generally identified themselves with some larger group—like the Mimbreno, Coyotero, Chiricahua,

An Apache warrior with war club and feathered hat *(Courtesy Arizona Historical Society, Tucson, Photo AHS 17746)*

Tonto, White Mountain, Aravaipa, Jicarilla, or Mescalero, but rarely shared any overall sense that they were "Apache."

Most raids were conducted by fewer than a dozen warriors, who slipped in as quietly as possible, stole what they could carry, and did their best to disappear without being seen. They avoided fighting on these plunder raids, partly because any death of an Apache warrior set in motion a deadly chain of revenge raiding. The leader of a raiding party that lost a warrior often faced criticism at home, and relatives of the dead warrior would demand retaliation. These revenge raids often involved large parties of warriors, and their purpose was to find the killer, or at least members of the killer's band or tribe. Sometimes, these revenge raids pitted one Apache band against another—setting off a cycle of killings. Usually, they were conducted against other groups. Raids for both material goods and revenge were central to the Apache culture, offering the surest route to respect and leadership. War leaders gained the respect of other warriors, and acquired the material goods that they gave away to other members of the band to secure support for their leadership. The raiding culture also helped keep the scattered Apache bands safe, since their enemies knew that killing an Apache would bring retaliation.

The arrival of the Spanish in the Southwest in the 1500s completely upset the Apache culture, economy, and relationships with other native peoples in the region—beginning an escalation of violence that would ultimately convulse the entire region. The Spanish quickly conquered the settled pueblo people who depended on easily destroyed crops and villages for their survival. As a result, the Tohono O'odham, Hopi, Zuni, and others fought several bloody battles but soon learned they could not defeat the Spanish. The Spanish tried to impose their Christian religion, provided livestock, and greatly escalated warfare with the Apache raiders. Many historians noted that before the arrival of the Spanish, the Apache relied more on trading than raiding in their dealings with more settled Indian peoples. But two things quickly increased the scope of warfare. First, the Spanish pressed other tribes into service in their attempt to destroy the Apache. Second, the Apache acquired horses from the Spanish, which transformed their mode of warfare. Suddenly, the raiding parties could cover hundreds of miles and return with great quantities of supplies—especially livestock. The price of leadership rose significantly—with the power and generosity of a leader measured in horses and cattle.

THE CYCLE OF VIOLENCE BEGINS

The arrival of the Spanish also greatly increased the cost and danger of raiding because the militaristic Spanish repeatedly mounted expeditions to recover stolen livestock. The Spanish often also captured Apache prisoners and sold them into slavery. The lethal Spanish response to the Apache raids triggered the Apache's own obligatory revenge raids. The on-again, off-again warfare between the Spanish and the Apache continued from 1590 through 1821, when Mexico won its independence from Spain. Sometimes, the Spanish pursued a policy of divide and conquer—pitting the Apache against the Comanche, or making peace with one band of Apache or another. These attempts at peace would bring relative quiet for several years but always broke down eventually. The Apache remained too economically dependent on raiding, and the Spanish too unwilling to pay the cost of peace with adequate gifts and rations. Generally, the Spanish got the worst of the struggle. Apache raiding effectively halted the northward extension of Spanish influence and alternately depopulated huge areas of Arizona, New Mexico, and northern Mexico. The empire that had easily conquered the sophisticated, militaristic civilizations of the Inca and the Aztec proved ineffectual against the Apache—who could strike an isolated location with hundreds of warriors and then vanish back into the mountains when any large force of soldiers gave chase. Most of the scattered Spanish successes in the struggle were won with the assistance of their Indian allies, rather than by the Spanish troops or colonial militias.

In the 1820s, The new Mexican government initially sought peace with the Apache, realizing it could ill afford to continue the war with the elusive, indomitable Apache—who had already proven themselves some of the finest guerrilla warriors in history.

"Terrifying are the mountains which they ascend, and the waterless deserts which they traverse in order to wear out their pursuers," wrote Antonio Barreiro in 1931, legal advisor to the province of Chihuahua. "They never lack calmness, even when taken by surprise when they have not a chance for defense. They fight until breath fails them and usually prefer death to surrender."

But the peace between the Mexicans and the Apache proved fleeting. Even at best, it was fragmentary, based on arrangements between individual towns and nearby bands. One 1837 massacre involving the Santa Rita Del Cobre Mimbreno Apache had far-reaching consequences—leading to the emergence of Mangas Coloradas, one of the greatest of all Apache diplomats and war leaders.

Mangas's group in 1837 was led by Juan Jose, a once-renowned warrior who purchased peace and enough liquor to keep himself intermittently stupefied by keeping his warriors from molesting several hundred miners and members of a Mexican penal colony at nearby Santa Rita Del Cobre, about 15 miles east of Silver City, New Mexico. Younger warriors such as Mangas objected to the arrangement and continued to raid other settlements in Mexico, but Juan Jose insisted that the Apache not harm the miners. The effects of the Apache raids elsewhere, however, inevitably undercut Juan Jose's tenuous peace. The Apache killed an estimated 5,000 Mexican settlers, forced the abandonment of 100 settlements, and largely depopulated northern Mexico between 1820 and 1835, according to one estimate. The unceasing Apache raids prompted the desperate governments of several Mexican provinces to offer a 100-peso bounty for the scalp of any Apache male and 50 pesos each for women and children. Scalp hunters turned in hundreds of scalps, and the policy put the Apache on the defensive for a time. But it ultimately spawned decades of torture and retaliation. It also doomed Juan Jose's arrangement with Santa Rita Del Cobre.

In 1837, American scalp hunter, trapper and adventurer James Johnson showed up in Santa Rita Del Cobre and convinced residents he could eliminate forever the Apache threat by a single terrible act of betrayal. So they invited Juan Jose's band to a great feast, plied

MANGAS COLORADAS

William Shakespeare would have appreciated the scope of Mangas Coloradas's character—and the cruel times and hopeless choices that trapped him. Mangas Coloradas, whose Apache name was Kan-da-zis-tlishi-en, displayed in his tempestuous life the character traits necessary for classic tragedy: vision, power, and a final, fatal flaw. His life brimmed with contradictions: He struggled to secure peace—but all his life waged war; he swore never to trust his enemies—but met his end under a white flag; he triumphed for half a century—but died with defeat already inevitable. His enemy—Captain John Cremony—left a vivid description of the 6' 6" tall chief:

> In truth, he was a wonderful man. His sagacious [wise] counsels partook more of the character of wide and enlarged statesmanship than those of any Indian of modern times. His subtle and comprehensive intellect enrolled and united the three principle tribes of Arizona and New Mexico in one common cause. The name Mangas Colorado was the tocsin [warning] of terror and dismay throughout a vast region of country, whose inhabitants existed by his sufferance . . . His head was enormously large, with a broad forehead, a large, aquiline nose, a most capacious mouth, and broad, heavy chin. His eyes were rather small, but exceedingly brilliant and flashing when under any excitement—although his outside demeanor was as imperturbable as brass.

Throughout Mangas Coloradas's eventful life, he was driven by the need to draw together the scattered powers of his people and solve the lethal puzzle posed by the unremitting encroachment of other, far more powerful cultures.

He first demonstrated a certain flair for drama when he decided to wear a bright red flannel suit taken as loot in a raid on a party of miners. He wore the shirt until it tattered into rags, by which time the rest of the band had begun calling him Mangas Coloradas ("Red Sleeves").

His second early departure from tradition proved more deadly. Mangas already had two Apache wives—a measure of his rising stature as a warrior. He then took a beautiful Mexican girl from the village of Janos as a third wife. The brothers of his first two wives objected and challenged him to a duel—he killed them both in a knife fight.

them with liquor, and then unveiled a great pile of food and gifts in the center of the village square. The Apache crowded forward eagerly, except for some wary warriors like Mangas who hung back and watched the greedy scramble with disdain. "They kept to the edges, watching," recalled James Kaywaykla, an Apache whose account was preserved by historian Eve Ball in *In The Days of Victorio.*

Suddenly, Johnson's men pulled the blankets off the cannons and opened fire on the mass of Indians in the center square. Slaughter ensued: Johnson himself shot down Juan Jose as the old chief turned to him in confusion, pleading for mercy. But Mangas and a handful of warriors escaped the slaughter. The Apache code disdains futile courage. Although Apache warriors fought with astonishing courage and desperation when trapped or mortally wounded, they thought it foolish and contemptible to waste the life of a warrior if escape was possible. Two of Mangas Coloradas's wives died in the first crash of cannon fire. But as Mangas fled, he scooped up a screaming baby—only later to discover it was his own son.

1837: MANGAS COLORADAS TAKES CHARGE

The other warriors turned naturally to Mangas for leadership. Surviving accounts suggest that hundreds of Apache died in the massacre—mostly women and children. Mangas took charge, as though born to leadership. Apache lead by force of character, moral example, and their spiritual power. Individual warriors remained fiercely independent, not bound by anyone's orders. Apache did not elect leaders, and leadership could not be inherited, only earned through great deeds, success in raiding, and generosity.

Mangas Coloradas forbade any immediate retaliation so that the miners would relax their guard. Then he sent couriers running to all of the nearby, related bands. Marshaling his forces, he laid ambushes along all of the routes leading into Santa Rita, tightening the noose on the celebrating Santa Rita. The miners didn't worry too much until the resupply train was a week late—then they sent out a well-armed group to investigate. The party never returned. Gradually, it dawned on the residents of Santa Rita that they'd made a terrible mistake. Low on food and ammunition, the entire settlement determined to make a dash for the next major Mexican settlement. But Mangas's warriors were waiting all along the route: Only a handful of the Santa Rita settlers survived. The Apache spared only the children—adopting them into their bands to replace their own murdered children. Mangas then set to work clearing his whole territory of Mexican settlers, unleashing a decades-long scourge that left him master of a great territory.

Mangas Coloradas consolidated his position in the fragmented political landscape of Apache culture like a European monarch marrying off princes and princesses. One of Mangas's daughters married Cochise, a highly respected Chiricahua Apache war leader. Others married the most prominent leaders of the Navajo and the Coyotero Apache.

The Apache generally held their own against Mexico, which was plagued by a corrupt, underfunded, poorly trained, poorly equipped military. In Apache territory, warriors and raiding parties usually moved freely while settlers kept to the areas around small towns and fortified garrisons. It was a remarkable achievement. The Apache fought both the Spanish Empire and Mexico to a standstill during nearly 150 years of constant warfare, generally expanding their influence, fighting capability, and strength throughout the period.

1846: THE ARRIVAL OF THE AMERICANS

But it couldn't last. The Americans were on the way. The Mimbreno Apache led by Mangas Coloradas first encountered the Americans during the Mexican-American War (1846–48). Warriors cautiously approached a U.S. Army column guided by the famous scout Kit Carson and commanded by General Stephen Watts

Kearny as it crossed Mangas's territory in 1846, maneuvering to cut off Mexico's northernmost possessions in the course of the Mexican-American War. First Lieutenant William Helmsley Emory described Mangas's warriors who offered to help the United States wage war on Mexico:

> A large number of Indians had collected about us, all dif-
> ferently dressed, and in some of the most fantastical
> style. The Mexican dress and saddles predominated,
> showing where they had chiefly made their wardrobe
> . . . Several wore beautiful helmets, decorated with black
> feathers, which, with the short skirt, waist belt, bare legs
> and buckskins, gave them the look of a picture of an-
> tique Greek Warriors. Their hills are covered with luxuri-
> ant gamma [grass], which enables them to keep their
> horse in fine order, so that they can always pursue with
> rapidity and retreat with safety. The light and graceful
> manner in which they mounted and dismounted always
> on the right side was the admiration of all.

Another officer, Captain A. R. Johnson, noted:

> They are partly clothed like Spaniards, with wide draw-
> ers, moccasins, and leggings to the knee; they carry a
> knife frequently in the right legging, on the outside;
> their moccasins have turned-up square toes, their hair is
> long, and mostly they have no headdress; some have fan-
> tastic helmets; they have some guns but mostly are
> armed with lances and bows and arrows. Just as we
> were leaving camp . . . an old Apache chief came in and
> harangued the General thus: "You have taken Santa Fe,
> let us go on and take Chihuahua and Sonora; we will go
> with you. You fight for the soil, we fight for plunder; so
> we will agree perfectly."

Kearny rebuffed Mangas's offer of alliance against the Mexicans but accepted his help in returning the column's horses and mules, which had a tendency to wind up in the possession of the warriors who shadowed the column as long as it remained in their territory.

1851: BORDER COMMISSION SPURS CONFLICT

The next major contact had a more ominous outcome. Congress dispatched a boundary commission to survey a new border between the United States and Mexico after the United States defeated Mexico in the Mexican-American War in 1848. The Apache and the Americans initially got along well, as notable Apache leaders like Mangas Coloradas came into the camp and sought a peaceful relationship. Captain John Cremony, who served as a scout and translator for the expedition, set up his tent apart from the soldiers and was soon thronged by Apache because he was one of the few Americans with whom they could communicate—he spoke Spanish as did many Apache.

These early American accounts of their encounters with the "savages" showed a mingling of fear, respect, and revulsion. Gripped by their "manifest destiny" to conquer the continent and wrest the wilderness away from the native people, most Americans believed implicitly in the racial, intellectual, and cultural superiority of the white race. Even relatively sympathetic observers of the Apache invariably colored their descriptions with the assumptions that the Apache were "savage" and virtually doomed to extinction. Wearing the blinders of racial attitudes, virtually all white observers agreed that the Apache should give way to the "higher" civilization, which could put the land to better use—through mining, logging, ranching, and construction.

"THE RED MAN DISDAINS MY HAND"

Cremony viewed the Apache with a mingling of disdain and admiration, and he recorded his observations in his book *My Life Among the Apaches*, which remains one of the few first-person accounts of these early contacts with the Apache.

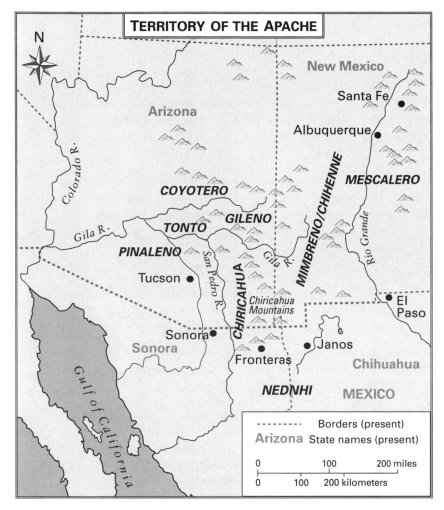

This map of the Southwest shows the territories of the major Apache groups based in mountain ranges in Arizona, New Mexico, and northern Mexico.

The Red Man . . . disdains to take my hand. He flouts my offered sympathy, and feels indigent at my presumption in proffering him my aid to improve his condition. He conceives himself not only my equal, but decidedly my superior. He desires only to be let alone. With calm and unruffled dignity he listens to all you say, and with unconcealed dislike he makes it a point to remember nothing he has heard. You are understood to

JOHN CREMONY

John Cremony was a man brimming with contradictions—exuberant, vain, insightful, untrustworthy, courageous, observant, narrow-minded, racist, and tolerant. His remarkable firsthand look at the Apache reveals the cultural arrogance that made that genocidal war possible. But it also offers a compelling picture of an ancient culture on the cusp of destruction, with a dash of flat-out adventure. Cremony shuttles between contempt and admiration for his "savage" adversaries, first as a translator for the international boundary commission in 1851, then as an officer in the Apache wars, and finally as an officer at a virtual concentration camp created for the Navajo and Apache at Bosque Redondo.

Cremony recounted one remarkable brush with death on a 96-mile journey between military posts. He was crossing a broad, barren plain on a treasured horse, when he saw a band of approaching Apache. He calmly tightened his saddle, loaded his guns, and tied a thick serape over his shoulders. He let the warriors draw to within 300 yards before he remounted his now rested horse and fled. He conserved his horse as much as possible, protected by the flapping serape, which caught several arrows. One arrow grazed his right arm, and one sliced across his left thigh. But he seemed safe enough, until he noted the warriors had abandoned the pursuit as the trail swept into a long curve.

"Suddenly, it flashed upon my mind that they might have some short cutoff, and had pursued it with the intention of heading me. For the first time I struck my rowels into the reeking flanks of my poor steed, and most gallantly did he respond to this last call."

The burst of speed put him about 80 yards ahead of where the Apache reentered the trail.

Cremony reported several other adventures in the next year, when he served as a guide for various parties of miners, soldiers, and adventurers. Once, he stumbled into an Apache ambush in a blinding sandstorm. The battle quickly degenerated into fierce, hand-to-hand fighting.

"I was just reloading a six-shooter, when a robust and athletic Apache, much heavier than myself, stood before me. The instant we met, he advanced upon me with a long and keen knife."

They grappled, straining for advantage. They fell and the Apache wound up on top, holding Cremony's knife hand, pinning the other arm beneath a knee, and prepared to plunge his own knife in the helpless Cremony's throat.

"Holding me down with a grasp of a giant against which all my struggles were wholly vain, he raised aloft his long, sharp knife, and said, 'The white-eyed man, you will soon be dead.' I thought as he did, and in a frightful moment made a hasty commendation of my soul to the Benevolent."

The warrior plunged his knife down toward his throat, but Cremony twisted aside and the knife penetrated only the earth. Desperately, Cremony sank his teeth into the Apache's hand. Unable to free his hand, the Indian released his grip on Cremony's pinioned knife hand in an effort to transfer his own knife to his free hand. Seizing the momentary opportunity, Cremony thrust his own dagger into his enemy's side.

Cremony spent the next 10 years in California and served in the Union Army. He was at the Battle of Apache Pass in 1862, and later became the Indians' champion and arbiter when more than 8,000 feuding Navajo and Apache found themselves forcibly confined to Bosque Redondo. Eventually, he returned to San Francisco where he wrote his book and resumed his newspaper career. Cremony died of tuberculosis in San Francisco in 1879.

be his natural enemy. While he frankly admits that you are better clothed, better fed, and better conditioned in all respects than he is, he as frankly and persistently refuses all overtures and invitations to adopt your style of life . . . No amount of cold, hunger, or thirst seems to have any appreciable effect upon an Apache. Whatever his sufferings, no complaint or murmur is ever heard to escape his lips, and he is always ready to engage in any enterprise which promises a commensurate reward. The cunning of the Apache is only equaled by his skill and the audacity with which he executes his projects, and every success is chuckled over with undissembled gusto by the whole tribe.

The American assumption of superiority and the pride of the Apache made a breakdown in the friendly relations between

Mangas's band and the boundary commission almost inevitable. The first open breech came when two Mexican children held captive by an Apache warrior came to Cremony's tent and pleaded for his help in returning home. The Apache protested the confiscation of their captives, according to Cremony's later recollection of the event, who reproduced it, complete with dialogue in *Life Among the Apaches*. "Why did you take our captives from us?" asked Mangas, baffled, his dignity offended. "Your captives came to us and demanded protection," returned Bartlett, who headed the American expedition to survey the new boundary between the United States and Mexico. "You came to our country, you were well received," returned Mangas sadly. "Your lives, your property, your animals were safe. You passed by ones, by twos, by threes through our country. You went and came in peace. Your strayed animals were always brought home to you again. Our wives, our women, and children, came here and visited you. We were friends—we were brothers! Believing this, we came among you and brought our captives, relying on it that we were brothers and that you would feel as we feel. We concealed nothing. We came in open day, and before your faces." After a tense standoff, Bartlett offered to ransom the boys with about $250 worth of trade goods. The Apache sullenly accepted the offer.

A second, more serious, incident occurred shortly thereafter. A Mexican packer got into a dispute with an Apache warrior and shot him. Mangas demanded that Bartlett turn over the packer. Bartlett refused, explaining that the man would be sent back to Santa Fe for trial. The commission's doctors labored to save the wounded warrior, but he died after several weeks. The Apache then renewed their demand that the commission hand over his murderer. Bartlett again refused, but he offered to pay the murdered man's family $20 per month. "But money will not satisfy an Apache for the blood of a brave," protested Mangas's son Ponce, according to Cremony's recollection. "Thousands will not drown the grief of this poor woman for the loss of her son. Would money satisfy an American for the murder of his people? No. I demand the blood of the murderer. Then I would be satisfied."

The incident signaled the end of the brief rapprochement between Mangas and the Americans. He left in anger and revoked his edict against stealing the commission's livestock. Soon, the soldiers lost nearly all of their horses, and after due reflection, decided to move their base of operations. However, the commission left behind an infestation of prospectors.

The encounter between Mangas's band and the boundary commission foretold the future. The initially friendly relations between the Americans and the Apache would give way to conflict, misunderstanding, and death. The Apache and Navajo, convinced that the Americans were just like the Mexicans, stole 12,000 mules, 7,000 horses, 31,000 cattle, and 45,000 sheep in New Mexico alone between 1846 and 1850. The Apache remained economically and culturally dependent on raiding, while the Americans appeared determined to wrest away from them the best hunting grounds without offering the Apache any alternative way to survive.

Meanwhile, even as the Americans pressured the Apache to stop raiding into Mexico, the Mexicans intensified their generations-long warfare with the Apache—extending the bounty for Apache scalps. The scalp trade peaked between 1849 and 1850. Notorious scalp hunter James Kirker and his men alone turned in 487 scalps in that period.

Observing that the Apache made it unsafe to travel 10 miles from Santa Fe, Agent James Calhoun recommended beginning a program to buy peace by feeding the raiders. "The thought of annihilating these Indians cannot be entertained by an American public—nor can the Indians abandon their predatory incursions . . . for no earthly power can prevent robbers and murderers unless the hungry wants of these people are provided for." Calhoun offered what proved a prophetic warning to his heedless superiors. "Expend your millions now [to] avoid the expenditures of millions hereafter." The most intelligent observers of the Apache issued prophetic warnings about what would become the chief American policy with regards to the Apache—forcing all the bands to settle on one or two barren reservations. "The policy of concentration is a pernicious one and can have but one result: It will stimulate their fondness for war," wrote John Bartlett after completing his boundary survey mission.

Chief Marco summed up the Apache dilemma when the Americans ordered his band to stop raiding into Mexico. "Have you, then, seen between the Pecos and the Lympia game enough to feed three thousand people? We have had for a long time no food to eat than the meat of Mexican cattle and mules, and we must make use of it still or perish. If you will give us cattle to feed our families, we will no longer take them from the Mexicans."

NOTES

p. 5   "Terrifying are the mountains . . ." Donald Worcester. *The Apaches: Eagles of the Southwest* (Norman: University of Oklahoma Press, 1979), p. 35.

p. 6   "In truth, he was a wonderful man . . ." Cremony, p. 49.

p. 9   "A large number of Indians . . ." Dan Thrapp. *Victorio and the Mimbres Apaches* (Norman: University of Oklahoma Press, 1974), p. 21.

p. 9   "They are partly clothed . . ." Worcester, p. 43.

pp. 11, 13 "The Red Man . . ." John Cremony. *Life Among the Apaches* (1868; reprint, Lincoln: University of Nebraska Press, 1983), p. 94.

p. 12   "Suddenly, it flashed . . ." Cremony, p. 77.

p. 12   "I was just reloading . . ." Cremony, p. 132.

p. 13   "Holding one down . . ." Cremony, p. 133.

p. 14   "Your captive came to us . . ." Cremony, p. 62.

p. 14   "But money will not satisfy . . ." Cremony, p. 69.

p. 15   "The thought of annihilating . . ." Worcester, p. 45.

p. 15   "Expend your millions now . . ." Worcester, p. 45.

pp. 15–16 "The policy of concentration . . ." Worcester, p. 45.

p. 16   "Have you, then, seen . . ." Worcester, p. 48

A TREACHEROUS DEATH

1860s

The conflict between the Americans and the Apache built gradually in the 1850s, driven by the economic needs of the Apache and the American conviction that these "savage" people must give way to the "superior" civilization. E. A. Graves, agent to the Mangas Coloradas's Mimbreno and Chihenne Apache noted:

> That this race, the aborigines of America, are destined to
> a speedy and final extinction, according to the laws now
> in force, either civil or Divine, seems to admit of no
> doubt, as is equally beyond the control of management
> of any human agency. All that can be expected from an
> enlightened and Christian government, such as ours, is
> to graduate and smooth the passway for their final exit
> from the state of human existence.

But Graves also realized that the Apache had little choice but to continue raiding:

> No animal creature, whether civilized or not, will perish
> for want of food when the means of subsistence are
> within his reach . . . to feed and clothe those Indians,
> either wholly or partially, is an expensive operation. It is
> a policy that promises no results beyond the simple fact

of keeping them quiet for the time being. . . . If you make
war on them and conquer them, the same question
arises: What to do with them? You will either have to
take care of them or destroy them.

Gripped by racist notions of superiority, few expressed any respect for native cultures. The hard-liners urged extermination, but even "reformers" wanted to "civilize" the Indians—by turning them into individual landowners, farmers, and Christians—thereby destroying their ancient cultures. Special Indian Agent Sylvester Mowrey observed:

> The end of these people, like that of all Indian tribes, is
> only a question of time. It is the duty of the government
> to preserve them, if possible, in their friendly attitude.
> The idea of civilizing and Christianizing them, exposed
> as they are to all the influences of a frontier people, is the
> idle dream of a pseudo-philanthropist. The rapid settle-
> ment of the territory will bring them soon into contact
> with the humanizing and civilizing influence of the
> white man and the result will be the inevitable one that
> has followed its contact with the tribes: the men will be-
> come drunkards, the women prostitutes, and disease
> will soon live only the name of their race . . . My own im-
> pression is that the Apaches cannot be tamed: civiliza-
> tion is out of the question. If these ideas shock any
> weak-minded individual who thinks himself a philan-
> thropist, I can only say . . . a man might as well have
> sympathy for a rattlesnake or a tiger.

Others expressed at least some understanding of the Apache's plight. Famed scout Kit Carson observed that violence fed on itself. "The Indians that are now committing depredations are those who have lost their families during the war. They consider they have nothing further to live for than revenge for the death of those of their families that were killed by whites; they have become desperate."

Raphael Pumpelly, a settler with mining interests, observed: "It is said that the Indians are treacherous and cruel, scalping and torturing their prisoners. It may be assured that there is no treachery and no cruelty left unemployed by the whites. Poisoning with strychnine, the willful dissemination of smallpox . . . these are the heroic facts among many of our frontiersmen."

Still, the Apache and the Americans avoided all-out war through most of the 1850s. The Americans sought fitfully to prevent Apache raiding, usually by providing sporadic supplies for bands settled near forts. The government's primary interest lay in protecting wagon routes through the Southwest, taking settlers from the East to the promised land of California. Generally, the bands whose territories were closest to these wagon routes came into the first and most persistent conflicts with the whites.

In New Mexico, that included the Mimbreno and Chihenne bands led by Mangas Coloradas, plus the Mescalero bands. In Arizona, that included the powerful Chiricahua Apache bands then led by Cochise—Mangas Coloradas's son-in-law and a rising force among the Apache. Both Cochise and Mangas Coloradas exerted their considerable powers to maintain peace with the Americans, knowing they couldn't fight a two-front war with both the Americans and the Mexicans. The Apache had long raided northern Mexico and retreated to rest into the wilderness of present-day New Mexico and Arizona.

However, the uneasy peace that prevailed through the 1850s shattered in the 1860s, in both Arizona and New Mexico. The accumulation of wrongs and the withdrawal of most soldiers as a result of the outbreak of the Civil War in 1861 combined to give the Apache their last, brief victory—a final chance to live the old life and triumph as warriors.

1861: MANGAS COLORADAS DRIVEN TO WAR

Mangas Coloradas searched for some way to deal with the Americans throughout the 1850s. The government dispatched Dr. Michael Steck to serve as Indian agent between 1855 and

1860, and he reported that Mangas urged his followers to cooperate with the Americans. Mangas Coloradas even led the way in planting crops, trying to help his band develop some food source besides continued raiding into Mexico.

But the relative quiet of Mangas's warriors only encouraged further encroachment. By 1860, perhaps 200 to 1,000 miners and settlers had set up operations in the heart of Mangas's territory—not far from the massacre site of 1837. Once again, Mangas pondered the best way to deal with the threat of the Americans and to somehow appease their insatiable demands.

"The lure of gold brought them to our home," said Ace Daklugie, the son of the famous Chiricahua war chief Juh whose recollections were recorded in *Indeh, an Apache Odyssey* by Eve Ball. "I have heard people say that self-preservation is the first law of life and that the perpetuation of the race is the second. That may be true of Indians, but getting something for nothing was the outstanding characteristic of White Eyes. We cared nothing for gold, yet it is thought that we are superstitious about it. That is not true. It is of little value, even for bullets. I've used both gold and silver ones, and neither is good. It is the White Eyes who are superstitious."

James Kaywaykla, another of Eve Ball's Apache informants, agreed: "It was the prospectors and miners we considered most objectionable, for they groveled in the earth and invoked the wrath of the Mountain Gods by seeking gold, the metal forbidden to man. It is a symbol of the sun, of Ussen Himself, and sacred to him."

Mangas decided to try to find some way to use the Americans' greed for gold to get them to leave his territory. So in 1861, Mangas went among the miners, taking them aside individually, and offering to lead them to much richer diggings. The miners compared notes and concluded that Mangas was trying to lure them to their deaths. Resolved to teach the chief a lesson, they waited until he returned and took him prisoner. They tied him to posts and ripped his back to ribbons with a bullwhip. The miners left him lashed to the head frame of a mine and his sons cut him down during the night. Mangas Coloradas then unleashed his warriors against the roughly 200 miners who had settled in the heart of their territory. Isolated hunting parties were killed, supply trains were ambushed, and miners killed. The Apache resorted to mutilations and torture, determined to avenge the humiliation of their leader. Usually, the Apache mutilated the bodies of their enemies after death, but now torture became more common. For hundreds of miles along trails leading through Mangas's domain, the slaughter continued—with prisoners sometimes suspended head down from a tree over a fire.

Mangas Coloradas called upon his network of allies to rid his territory of the Americans. Both Cochise and the Navajo chief Francisco had married Mangas Coloradas's daughters, so they helped the great chief in his bitter war with the whites. The vengeful warriors soon cleared the territory of miners and made it unsafe for any but the most vigilant and heavily armed parties. Mangas Coloradas thought that he had won a great victory, but his offensive had coincided with the onset of the Civil War, which had forced the Union to withdraw most of its troops from the Southwest.

1861: COCHISE GOES TO WAR

The first American settlers found southeast Arizona dominated by the Chiricahua Apache and three or four closely related groups led by one of the most remarkable and successful of Apache leaders—Cochise. The Apache concept of authority and leadership differed sharply from the hierarchical, top-down concepts of the Americans; Apache leaders relied on personal example and every warrior retained complete freedom and autonomy. Each leader displayed his own distinctive style and exercised leadership only so long as he succeeded.

"Leadership styles were as varied as the individuals who attracted followings," observed historian D. C. Cole in *The*

*Chirica*hua Apaches. "Mangas Coloradas led by long and skill-fully handled discussions in which superior diplomacy and weight of argument caused his own counsel to prevail. Cochise led by sheer integrity and moral example. Geronimo held his followers by enigmatic behavior and examples of raw Power. Victorio was successful as long as his sister Lozen's war Power sustained him. Juh, inhibited by a speech impediment, let other people speak for him. Ulanza led by dash and Nana by stealth. Each had his followers."

Cochise certainly ranks as one of the best known and most successful of all Indian leaders. Feared and revered by his warriors, he was a dignified, somber, noble character in a doomed cause. His Apache name was Cheis, meaning "oak." A fierce warrior, expert marksman, peerless horseman, and brilliant strategist—he spent his whole life fighting the Mexicans and Americans. He was repeatedly wounded, captured once by the Mexicans, and forever hunted—but he died of natural causes as an old man. He was a ruthless, gifted, often cruel warrior—single-minded in his devotion to the survival of his people. His biographer Edwin Sweeney details the long, deadly series of battles Cochise fought against the Mexicans before the Americans arrived on the scene in the 1850s. Like most Apache leaders, Cochise initially saw the Americans as potential allies against the Mexicans.

Even when the insightful Cochise begin to appreciate the threat the inrushing Americans presented, he took care to maintain peace with them in the heart of the Chiricahua territory—the spectacularly rugged Chiricahua and Dragoon Mountains in southwestern Arizona. These inaccessible mountain ranges had for generations provided the Chiricahua Apache with a splendid fortress and year-round supplies of food and water. Lookouts could see the approach of enemies by their dust clouds 40 miles away, giving the warriors a full day to either prepare their defenses or an ambush. Cochise initially sought to enforce peace by forbidding attacks on settlers, wagon trains, troops, and couriers. He even supplied the stage station in Apache Pass with wood. But in February of 1861, an inexperienced army lieutenant named

Mickey Free, the half-Apache, half-Mexican shown here, was kidnapped by the Apache as a child, triggering the decade-long war between Cochise and the Americans. He was later raised by the Apache and served as a translator for General Crook and Britton Davis. *(Courtesy Arizona Historical Society, Tucson, Photo AHS 1153)*

George Bascom ignited a spark that would set a wildfire that would burn for a decade—claiming hundreds of lives.

A local rancher complained to the army that Apache had kidnapped his adopted son—a half-Mexican, half-Apache boy later known as Mickey Free. At that time, most Americans knew so little about the Apache that they believed the many independent bands were a single tribe led by Cochise. Lieutenant Bascom led a detachment of 54 soldiers to Apache Pass, a stage station in the heart of Cochise's territory, and invited Cochise to parlay. The unsuspecting Cochise brought his brother, two nephews, a woman, and two children to the army tent. Bascom demanded the return of the kidnapped boy. Cochise explained that he had no idea who had taken the boy but would try to get the boy returned. Bascom then ordered the seven Apache seized. Reacting instantly, Cochise whipped out his knife, slashed a hole in the wall of the tent, and ran to freedom through the astonished guards. The soldiers fired some 50 shots and wounded Cochise in the leg, but he reached the top of a nearby hill still clutching the coffee cup from which he'd been drinking. He returned a short while later, calling from the hilltop for permission to speak to his imprisoned brother. Bascom answered with a volley of gunfire. "I will be avenged," shouted Cochise from the hilltop. "Indian blood is as good as white man's blood."

Cochise dispatched his warriors to take hostages to exchange for his imprisoned relatives, seizing two stagecoach employees. Cochise then offered to exchange his prisoners and 16 mules for his family and friends. Bascom refused. The aroused Chiricahua warriors attacked stage coaches and killed eight Mexican teamsters—lashing them to wagon wheels and burning their bodies. Meanwhile, a relief column arrived—bringing three Coyotero Apache prisoners. Ultimately, Cochise gave up negotiating and killed his prisoners—mutilating their bodies. The soldiers found the butchered bodies and retaliated by hanging six of their prisoners—including Cochise's brother. The tragic incident ignited a decade of all-out war between Cochise and the Americans.

1861–72: COCHISE EXACTS REVENGE

Cochise exacted a terrible revenge. His band killed an estimated 200 whites in the next two months. He dragged prisoners to death behind his warhorse, watched as travelers were tortured to death or terribly mutilated after death, and drove most of the whites out of his territory. Initially, the twin wars of Cochise and Mangas Coloradas seemed to promise the return of the old days. The Apache chiefs didn't realize that much of their success sprang from the lack of troops in the West as a result of the outbreak of the Civil War in 1861. They believed that their raids forced the abandonment of most of the hated American forts, when it was actually the insatiable demand for troops to feed into the cannons in the East where Americans waged war on a lethal scale almost unimaginable to the Apache—who considered any raid in which a single warrior died a failure.

But the Apache victory proved short-lived. The Apache soon found themselves caught between two new forces—the Confederate Army pushing into New Mexico from the East in early 1861 and the Union Army pushing into Arizona from California in 1862.

The Confederate forces entered the area under the command of Lieutenant Colonel John Baylor, who in 1861 ordered the immediate extermination of the Apache. He told his troops to kill any warriors and to sell the women and children as slaves to defray the cost of the campaign. Confederate president Jefferson Davis later countermanded the order, and the Confederates never made much headway against the Apache and were soon driven out of the Southwest by the Union forces.

The incoming Union forces posed a more persistent problem. Cochise learned that a large army composed of nearly 3,000 Union troops from California had entered his territory in 1862, and he called upon his father-in-law and other Apache allies to raise one of the greatest forces in the history of Apache warfare. The combined force included the leaders who were to dominate the conflict for the next two decades, including Victorio, his sister Lozen, Nana, Kaytennae, and other leaders of the Mimbreno and Chihenne Apache, and leaders who rose to prominence among the Chiricahua including Juh and an obscure but rising war leader named Geronimo, who was not a chief but whose courage, daring, and spiritual powers made him a potent leader in battle.

Cochise and Mangas Coloradas mustered 200 to 700 warriors—estimates vary wildly—and laid plans to ambush the leading detachment of the California Volunteers at Apache Pass on July 15, 1862. Cochise knew the soldiers would approach water there after crossing 40 miles of desert in the blazing summer sun. The Apache warriors hid on a rocky hillside overlooking the spring and waited for the detachment of about 68 soldiers, hauling two mysterious metal cylinders mounted on wheels. Just behind, a supply train that included 242 animals guarded by 45 soldiers offered the alluring possibility of plunder. These two detachments constituted the advance contingent of more than 2,300 under the command of Colonel James Carleton.

The trap was spoiled when a band of warriors swooped down on the supply train, tipping the soldiers to the Apache presence. No matter, thought the waiting warriors; the soldiers must still come forward for the water, or turn and survive a waterless, 40-mile trek back to Dragoon Springs. But instead of rushing the spring, the soldiers brought their two, twelve-pounder cannons to bear on the Apache fortifications above the spring. The lopsided battle lasted for about three hours. The Apache warriors killed two soldiers and wounded two more. The American commander claimed nine Apache dead. Descendants of warriors who fought there claim that no Apache warriors died.

Nonetheless, the battle was decisive. It marked the last time the Apache tried to mass their forces against American soldiers. The Apache leaders realized that they could never win such large-scale battles because of the soldiers' immense superiority in both firepower and numbers.

The battle brought one additional disaster. The besieged soldiers in Apache Pass sent a small detachment of men riding back toward the main column to bring up reinforcements. About 20 warriors under Mangas's leadership rode in pursuit, cutting off one trooper when Mangas brought down the trooper's horse. Trooper John Teal later recounted the standoff and a fateful shot:

> My horse fell, and as I approached him, he began to lick my hands. I then swore to kill at least one Apache. Lying down behind the body of my dying animal, I opened fire upon them with my carbine—which being a breech-loader enabled me to keep up a lively fire. This repeated fire seemed to confuse the savages, and instead of advancing with a rush they commenced to circle around me, firing occasional shots in my direction. In this way the fight continued for over an hour, when I got a good chance at a prominent Indian and slipped a carbine ball into his breast. He must have been a man of some note, because soon after that I could hear their voices growing fainter in the distance.

Teal had hit Mangas Coloradas. The warriors hurried Mangas to Janos, a Mexican city with which they maintained friendly relations. "The Apaches feared that the White Medicine Man might kill their chief instead of curing him, but they took the risk," Daklugie later told historian Eve Ball in *Indeh*. "They warned the Medicine Man that if Mangas Coloradas died, they would kill every person in the village. He recovered."

But the old chief had come to understand the hopelessness of the Apache struggle. In his seventies, Mangas realized that his desperate struggle of half a century had only delayed the inevitable. Again and again, he'd proven himself as a warrior. Again and again, he'd exacted terrible vengeance. Now, he realized that he must risk everything to secure some sort of peace for his people. Extermination remained the only alternative.

1863: MESCALERO APACHE ARE BROKEN

Mangas Coloradas's allies the Mescalero Apache were next to face a concentrated army campaign. General Carleton, an efficient, self-righteous, determined man, made scout Kit Carson a colonel and ordered him to hunt down the Mescalero. "The Indians are to be soundly whipped, without parleys or councils," Carleton ordered. "All Indian men of that tribe are to be killed whenever and where ever you can find them. The women and children will not be harmed, but you will take them prisoners, and feed them at Fort Stanton until you receive instructions about them. I think that this severity in the long run will be the most humane course that could be pursued against these Indians."

Dr. Michael Steck, the civilian agent to the Mescalero, Mimbreno, and Chihenne, argued staunchly against the campaign. He insisted that the Apache had maintained the peace between 1854 and 1860 but had been driven to hostilities by the specter of starvation. Steck noted that the $3 million annual cost of the military campaign was 20 times what it would take to keep the Mescalero settled on a reservation by providing sufficient food. "It needs no prophetic eye to see that in a few years the Indians of New Mexico must be exterminated, unless the government interposes its benevolent hand to protect and support them," wrote Steck. But the pleas of the peacemakers once more fell on deaf ears. In part, that was because the settlers and the local newspapers repeatedly raised an outcry against the Indians. Moreover, contractors who benefited from that $3 million in annual military expenditures lobbied against peace at every opportunity.

General John Pope noted: "What the white man does to the Indian is never known. It is only what the Indian does to the white man (nine times out of ten in the way of retaliation) which reaches the public." The starving Indians are "driven to the necessity of warring to the death upon the white man, whose inevitable and destructive progress threatens total extermination of the Indians." Carson's campaign against the Mescalero was short, brutal, and effective. On several occasions, Carson ignored his order and allowed warriors to surrender. However, the campaign also included several incidents in which soldiers fired on bands attempting to surrender.

"YOU ARE STRONGER THAN WE"

Cadete, the leading Mescalero chief, eventually surrendered the starving remnants of his people to Carleton in November of 1862 and spoke of the desperation of the Apache. Carleton's aide recorded Cadete's surrender speech.

> You are stronger than we. We have fought you so long as we had rifles and powder; but your weapons are better than ours. Give us like weapons and turn us loose, we will fight you again; but we are worn out; we have no more heart; we have no provisions, no means to live; your troops are everywhere; our springs and water holes are either occupied or overlooked by your men. You have driven us from our last and best stronghold, and we have no more heart. Do with us as may seem good to you, but do not forget that we are men and braves.

Carleton sent some 350 Mescalero to the barren expanse of Bosque Redondo, a virtual prison camp on the banks of the Rio Grande. He ordered Carson to apply the same medicine to the Navajo, who proved more vulnerable than the Apache because they relied on their herds, farms, and orchards. Carson burned their orchards, destroyed their fields, and took their herds—soon reducing the Navajo to starvation. Most surrendered, and Carleton settled 8,000 Navajo at Bosque Redondo as well.

Conflict between the Navajo and the Mescalero soon drove the Apache to flee the reservation and return to their homeland in New Mexico, where they were allowed to settle and given rations.

The Navajo remained at Bosque Redondo until 1868, when they too were allowed to return to their homeland. In addition, the Americans tried to address one of the major reasons that the Apache and the Navajo continued to raid. In June of 1865, President Andrew Johnson had finally outlawed the sale of Indians as slaves in New Mexico, attempting to halt a practice reaching back for generations, which had been ended in the rest of the country during the Civil War. But the decree actually did little to change the status of the estimated 2,000 Apache and Navajo slaves in New Mexico, nor to prevent the Mexicans from continuing to sell Apache slaves just across the border.

JANUARY 1863: AN ACT OF TREACHERY

Mangas Coloradas had returned to his home territory after his recovery from the wounds received at the battle of Apache Pass in July of 1862. In January 1863, he decided to seek peace with a party of Americans camped near Santa Rita where Mangas's long struggle with the whites had started. He went alone under a white flag to talk to the Americans, over the vehement objections of the other chiefs. The party of prospectors under the leadership of Joseph Reddeford Walker immediately seized the old chief and said that they would keep him prisoner to assure their safe passage through Apache territory. A short while later, they encountered a patrol led by Captain E. D. Shirland, who took their prisoner. General Carleton had ordered the extermination of all Apache warriors, and Shirland was anxious to produce this most valuable of prisoners. He turned Mangas Coloradas over to Colonel John West. This is the most widely reported version of this key event. The official army reports make no mention of the prospectors who initially seized the old chief.

Official army reports say Mangas Coloradas was shot after repeated escape attempts. However, a soldier later revealed that Colonel John West said to the guards: "That old murderer has got away from every command and has left a trail of blood for 5,000 miles on the old stage line. I want him dead or alive tomorrow morning, do you understand? I want him dead."*

Daniel Ellis Conner, walking sentry duty for the prospectors, reported seeing Mangas Coloradas's guards heating their bayonets and placing them against the great chief's feet and legs. At last, Mangas Coloradas protested and the soldiers shot him—and worse. The soldiers buried him the next day, but then dug him up, cut off his head, and boiled it in a great black pot. His skull later wound up in the Smithsonian, where phrenologist Orson Squire Fowler pronounced his cranial capacity greater then Daniel Webster's—a statistic that amazed many since the now-discredited theories of phrenology equated cranial capacity with intelligence.

"To an Apache, the mutilation of the body is much worse than death, because the body must go through eternity in that mutilated condition," Daklugie told historian Eve Ball in *Indeh*. "Little did White Eyes know what they were starting when they mutilated Mangas Coloradas. While there was little mutilation previously, it was nothing compared to what was to follow."

But the personal tragedy of Mangas Coloradas had run its course. He had struggled all his life to find a space for his people to survive and probably enjoyed more success than did any other Apache leader, but he died under a flag of truce, seeking a solution to the problem of coexistence.

The void left by the death of Mangas Coloradas was soon filled by a remarkable war leader named Victorio, a Chihenne or Warm Springs Apache—one of the major divisions of the group generally referred to as Mimbreno. Victorio kept his Chihenne band mostly out of the fighting. His group included the already elderly but indomitable war chief Nana, Victorio's warrior sister Lozen, and three sons of Mangas Coloradas. Victorio skillfully evaded Carson's roundup, rejecting any terms that would require his

---

* The incident remains controversial because eyewitness accounts disagree with official army accounts. Most historians accept the version offered by Conner, who was with the party of prospectors who originally captured Mangas Coloradas who stood sentry duty nearby the night Mangas was murdered.

band to abandon its homeland—Ojo Caliente near the Arizona–New Mexico border. But Carleton refused to consider any reservation other than Bosque Redondo, and Victorio's band faded back into the mountains. The Americans didn't worry much about it at the time, but they would hear more of the Chihenne warriors Victorio, Lozen, and Nana in a few years—to their deep regret.

1871: MASSACRE BOOSTS PEACEMAKERS

In the meantime, Cochise also found the cost of his battle with the Americans unendurable as the unremitting warfare claimed the lives of most of his warriors. Fortunately, the Americans had also wearied of the struggle. In addition, a massacre of mostly women and children finally aroused sympathy for the Apache in the East.

Several hundred Aravaipa Apache in February of 1871, wearying of constant warfare and near starvation, surrendered to Lieutenant Royal Whitman who was then in temporary command of Camp Grant—a dreary, forsaken wilderness outpost at the mouth of Aravaipa Canyon in eastern Arizona. The Aravaipa, led by a renowned war chief named Eskiminzin, placed themselves under the protection of the soldiers at the fort. But settlers in Tucson blamed the Aravaipa for continued raids and murders near Tucson. On April 30, 1871, a mixed group of Americans, Mexicans, and Tohono O'odham Indians attacked the Apache encampment, clubbing somewhere between 86 and 150 people to death—mostly women and children. The attackers raped or mutilated many of their victims, and took many children as prisoners for later sale as slaves. The massacre would ultimately raise an outcry that provided a rare opening for the peacemakers.

The national attention paid to the massacre had just begun to build when another event made national headlines—the death of one of the most famous of the Apache's foes, Lieutenant Howard Bass Cushing. He was ambushed by Nednhi Apache war chief Juh

Thomas Jeffords was Cochise's only friend among the whites and is shown here in retirement at his ranch north of Tucson. He played a key role in making peace between Cochise and the Americans, and he later served as Indian Agent to the Chiricahua reservation. *(Courtesy Arizona Historical Society, Tucson, Photo AHS 8170)*

in a canyon in southeastern Arizona in May of 1871. These two events coincided with the election to the presidency of General Ulysses S. Grant, who had become a national hero by leading the Union armies to victory. The Camp Grant massacre, the death of Cushing, and the growing pro-Apache sentiment in the East generally led by former abolitionists produced an emergence of a "peace policy."

Fortunately, Cochise had left one door open. He had made one exception to his decade-long war against the whites. The relationship between Cochise and a tall, red-headed, soft-spoken man named Thomas Jeffords represents a remarkable bridge between two warring cultures. Jeffords arrived in Arizona territory in 1862, and he ran the mail service between Tucson and Fort Bowie, which constantly lost riders to the Apache. Several conflicting versions of Jeffords's relationship to Cochise survive. In the most often repeated version, Jeffords rode alone to meet with Cochise into the Dragoon Mountains, an area even the army avoided. Apparently impressed by Jeffords's courage, Cochise let him enter the

ESKIMINZIN AND WHITMAN: FRIENDS AGAINST ALL ODDS

The great-hearted, ill-fated relationship between Lieutenant Royal Whitman and Aravaipa Apache chief Eskiminzin stands as one of the noble failures of the peacemakers in the long history of the Apache wars. Whitman was a New Englander with a stern conscience, who arrived at Camp Grant in 1870, assuming command of the straggling collection of tents and ramshackle adobe buildings at the unwalled camp in hopes of fighting Indians. Instead, starving Aravaipa Apache begin straggling into the camp, begging for army protection from bands of settlers.

Aravaipa Apache chief Eskiminzin had earned a fierce reputation as a war leader, but he soon saw the hopelessness of the struggle against the Americans. Throughout his eventful life, he remained a leading advocate for peace. Several hundred Aravaipa soon settled in around Camp Grant. Whitman encouraged them to plant crops and paid them for hay and firewood while he pleaded with Washington for official permission to establish a reservation for them there.

Settlers in Tucson fumed. Contractors complained that they suffered heavy financial losses when the army post begin buying supplies from the Apache instead of the contractors. Settlers blamed every raid, horse theft, and murder in the region on the Aravaipa, although other bands continued to raid in the area. Eventually, the settlers decided to take matters into their own hands. On April 30, 1871, William Oury gathered together a force of 94 Tohono O'odham Indians, 48 Mexicans, and five white settlers and attacked Eskiminzin's camp at dawn, killing between 85 and 150 Apache, only 8 of them men. They also seized many children and sold them into slavery.

The horrified Whitman came upon the scene of the slaughter a short time later. The soldiers fed and tended the survivors, and they buried the victims. Eskiminzin soon returned, having been off hunting with most of his warriors at the time of the massacre. "I no longer want to live," Eskiminzin said to Whitman. "But I will live to show those people who have done this to us that they have done all they can do but they shall not make me break faith with you so long as you stand by us and defend us . . . The people of Tucson must be crazy. They acted as though they had neither heads nor hearts . . . they must have a thirst for our blood . . . These Tucson people write for the papers and tell their own story. The Apaches have no one to tell their story."

Unfortunately, soldiers fired on Eskiminzin's survivors a short time later, apparently by mistake. Eskiminzin's band fled. But before he left, Eskiminzin visited another longtime white friend—rancher Charles McKinney. They ate, talked, shared a smoke. Then Eskiminzin killed McKinney. Later Eskiminzin explained that he murdered McKinney to demonstrate to his people that they could never be friends with the whites: "Any coward can kill his enemy, but it takes a brave man to kill his friend."

Eskiminzin eventually returned to the San Carlos Reservation established to contain many, often warring bands. There he continued his efforts to maintain peace between the Apache and the whites. He became a successful rancher and farmer, but settlers ultimately stole his land and he wound up imprisoned for killing McKinney.

Whitman also suffered for his attempt to seek justice. He testified against the people who perpetrated the Camp Grant massacre, but a civilian jury quickly acquitted them and then thanked the vigilantes for their service. Hated throughout the territory, Whitman underwent repeated court martials on trumped-up charges and left the army under a cloud.

But when General Howard met with Eskiminzin in 1871 attempting to fashion a peace policy, he asked Eskiminzin whether they could be friends. "Could I not come into your lodges at any time," asked the pious Howard, "even when you are on the warpath?" Eskiminzin replied, "Not unless you want to be killed." Taken aback, Howard asked, "Then what white man could visit you at any time?" Eskiminzin gestured toward Whitman. "Only one."

Dragoons where the two fearless, strong-willed men developed a remarkable friendship. However, other evidence suggests that Jeffords actually first met Cochise in about 1870, well after he'd quit running the mail service. At that time, Jeffords was a trader, selling goods to the Indians. He either went alone into the Dragoons to seek permission from the still warring Cochise to do business with the Apache or was captured and spared because Cochise was impressed with his courage. In any case, the slender thread of friendship was to prove vital in ending the warfare between Cochise and the Americans.

VINCENT COLYER SEEKS PEACE

President Grant sent a series of envoys with sweeping powers to negotiate with the warring Apache after his election in 1868. He first dispatched Vincent Colyer, with instructions to set aside reservations for as many groups as possible.

Colyer faced strenuous opposition in the West, where most of the settlers wanted the Apache exterminated. In addition, Colyer soon discovered that he faced the powerful political opposition of a network of contractors whose principle business lay in either selling supplies to the army or whisky and arms to the Apache. "Almost all of the paying business the white inhabitants have in the territory is in supplying the troops," noted General Edward Ord. "The Apaches have few friends. There seems to be no settled policy but only a general idea to kill them wherever found." Settlers generally greeted Colyer with cries of indignation and treason, insisting that advocates for peace were traitors to their own race who romanticized and misjudged the "savages" only because they lived so far from the scenes of torture, murder, and carnage.

Nonetheless, Colyer's mission produced results. He met with White Mountain, Coyotero, Mescalero, Mimbreno, and Chihenne Apache groups, generally setting aside reservations that included their traditional territories, persuading them to settle near forts, and promising to provide rations as an inducement to convince them to stop raiding into Mexico. Cochise also met with Colyer, but Colyer could not convince him to forsake the Dragoons and Chiricahua Mountains and settle with the Mimbreno near Ojo Caliente.

1872: GENERAL HOWARD MEETS WITH COCHISE

President Grant next dispatched General O. O. Howard in 1872 to make peace with Cochise. A courageous, fundamentalist, Howard had lost an arm in the Civil War, met with many Indian groups, generally winning their respect. Howard asked Jeffords to lead him into Cochise's stronghold. Jeffords agreed, providing they went alone, without soldiers. Jeffords convinced two members of Cochise's band to let them into the stronghold. Howard recalled waiting all night, uncertain whether he would be greeted or executed in the morning but drawing reassurance when several Apache children napped on his blanket. The next morning, Cochise rode into his camp, according to Howard's later recollection preserved in *Famous Indian Chiefs I Have Known*:

> As I took his hand, I remembered my impression. A man fully six feet in height, well proportioned, large dark eyes, face slightly painted with vermilion, unmistakably an Indian: Hair straight and black with a few silver threads, touching the coat collar behind. He gave me a grasp of the hand and said very pleasantly, "Buenos dias." His face was really pleasant to look upon, making me say to myself, "How strange it is that such a man can be the robber and murderer so much complained of." In my frequent interviews afterward, I perceived that when conversing upon all ordinary matters he was exceedingly pleasant, exhibiting a child like simplicity; but in touching upon the wrongs of the Apaches, in public council, or on horseback, in fact, when he considers himself to be specifically on duty as the Chirichua Chief, he is altogether another man.

Cochise spoke eloquently of the struggle of his people and bitterly of the army treachery at Apache Pass.

> We were once a large people, covering these mountains. We lived well, we were at peace. One day my best friend was seized by an officer of the white men and

CUSHING AND JUH

Nednhi Apache chief Juh and Captain Howard Cushing dedicated their lives to killing one another but had more in common than they would ever confess.

Juh remains the more important and mysterious figure, one of the greatest strategists and leaders in a culture that glorified the warrior and was consumed by war. Six feet tall, 225-muscled pounds, stocky and heavyset, Juh suffered all his life from a stutter that should have handicapped him in the war councils of the Apache where eloquence was prized. "Juh was very large, not fat, but stockily built. His heavy hair was braided and the ends fell almost to his knees. His features . . . were what people now call Mongoloid," reported James Kaywaykla, a young Apache warrior. Juh's prowess in war, the brilliance of his strategy, and his reputation among the Apache for the power to see the future and handle men won for him devoted followers. Juh led the Apache in many of their most famous battles, and he often defied the conventions of Apache warfare by fighting at night or sometimes charging enemy positions.

Cushing was his perfect foe. One of four war hero brothers, Cushing proved one of the most driven, successful, and relentless of Indian fighters. "An officer of wonderful experience in Indian warfare, who had killed more savages of the Apache tribe than any other officer or troop of the United States Army has done before or since," wrote Captain John Bourke. "He was about five feet seven in height, spare, sinewy, active as a cat; slightly stoop-shouldered, sandy complexioned, keen gray or bluish-gray eyes, which looked you through. When he spoke, he gave a slight hint of the determination and coolness and energy which had made his name famous all over the Southwestern Border." Determined, ambitious, and daring, Cushing adopted the task of tracking down and killing Cochise as a personal quest, in 1870 and 1871.

Juh's son, Ace Daklugie, later told historian Eve Ball that Juh decided to hunt down and entrap Cushing. Finally, they came together at Bear Springs Canyon in May of 1871. Cushing's scouts followed the tracks of a single Apache woman into the canyon. Veteran Sergeant John Mott led the advanced detachment. Suddenly, warriors emerged on both sides of the advanced detachment, wounding one private and killing the horse of a second. Incredibly, one warrior rode into the midst of the embattled soldiers and snatched the hat from a private's head—a virtuoso act of Apache daring. Mott noted that a heavyset Indian directed the battle with hand signals, Juh's hallmark.

Just as Juh planned, Cushing charged to the rescue with the rest of his 22-man force. The Apache faded into the rocks. Cushing brushed aside Mott's warnings and ordered a charge. "Cushing was so sure of himself and had killed so many Apaches, that he must have thought he knew more than Ussen Himself," Daklugie said later. Before the troop had covered 20 yards, the Apaches emerged again from the rocks. "It was as though every rock and bush had become an Indian," wrote Mott later. Mott heard Cushing cry out, "Sergeant, Sergeant, I am killed. Take me out! Take me out!"

Mott and another man begin dragging Cushing back down the canyon, but within 10 paces, another bullet struck Cushing in the face. The soldiers turned to make their stand, determined to "sell their lives dearly." But the Apache let the rest of the troop escape. "Juh wasn't much interested in the troops—just Cushing," Daklugie said. "Other White Eyes were killed too, I don't know how many. We weren't all the time counting the dead as the soldiers did."

Bourke bitterly mourned the passing of one of the west's most daring Indian fighters. "There is an alley named after him in Tucson," he wrote, "and there is, or was, when I last saw it, a tumbledown, worm-eaten board to mark his grave, and that was all to show where the great American nation had deposited the remains of one of its bravest."

treacherously killed . . . The worst place of all is Apache Pass. There five Indians, one my brother, were murdered. Their bodies were hung up and kept there till they were skeletons. Now Americans and Mexicans kill an Apache on sight. I have retaliated with all my might. My people have killed Americans and Mexicans and taken their property. Their losses have been greater than mine. I have killed 10 white men for every Indian slain, but I know that the whites are many and the Indians are few. Apaches are growing less every day . . . why shut me up on a reservation? We will make peace; we will keep it faithfully. But let us go around free as Americans do. Let us go where ever we please . . . When I was young, I walked all over this country, east, and west, and saw no other people than the Apaches. After many summers, I walked again and found another race of people who had come to take it. How is it? Why is it that the Apaches want to die—that they carry their lives on their fingernails? They roam over the hills and plains and want the heavens to fall on them. The Apaches were once a great nation, they are now but a few . . . Many have been killed in battle. Tell me, if the Virgin Mary has walked throughout all the land, why has she never entered the lodge of the Apache?

Howard initially tried to win Cochise's agreement to move his tribe to New Mexico, but Cochise stubbornly held out for a reservation that included the Dragoons. Howard eventually relented. Cochise kept the peace he promised until his death in 1874, wracked with pain from what historians suspect was either stomach or colon cancer. He saw his old friend Jeffords once shortly before he died. Jeffords had served as agent to the Chiricahua reservation, sometimes dipping into his own funds to augment the rations when the contractors short-changed him and enduring fierce public criticism because he could not curb continued Chiricahua raiding into Mexico.

Hearing that Cochise lay gravely ill, Jeffords hurried to visit him. Cochise predicted that he and the only white man he trusted would meet again. "Where?" asked Jeffords. "That I do not know. Somewhere. Up yonder, I think," replied the dying chief.

After he died, his warriors dropped Cochise's body into a great chasm in the Dragoons, along with his favorite horse, his favorite dog, a beautiful red woolen robe, and his combination rifle/shotgun with gold and silver inlay. Then they left his tomb, with wild cries of grief—taking care to ride their horses back and forth across the trail they'd left so that no one could defile his resting place. "The howl that went up from these people was fearful to listen to," recounted one observer of the way in which the grief spread from band to band. "They were scattered around in the nooks and ravines in parties, and as the howling from one rancheria would lag, it would be renewed with vigor in another. This was kept up through the night and until daylight the next morning."

NOTES

pp. 17–18   "That this race . . ." *Report of the Secretary of the Interior. 1854*, p. 389.

p. 18   "The end of these people . . ." *Report of the Secretary of the Interior. 1854*, p. 391.

p. 18   "My own impression . . ." *Report of the Secretary of the Interior. 1857*, p. 724.

pp. 18–19   "The Indians that are now . . ." *Report of the Secretary of the Interior. 1855*, p. 512.

p. 18   "It is said that the Indians . . ." Raphael Pumpelly. *Pumpelly's Arizona*, edited by Andrew Wallace (Tucson: University of Arizona Press, 1965), p. 350.

p. 20   "It was the prospectors . . ." Eve Ball. *In The Days of Victorio*. (Tucson: University of Arizona Press, 1970), p. 92.

p. 24   "I will be avenged . . ." David Roberts. *Once They Moved Like the Wind* (New York: Touchstone Books, 1993), p. 23.

p. 27   "My horse fell . . ." Cremony, p. 160.

p. 28   "The Indians are to be soundly whipped . . ." Edwin Sabin. *Kit Carson Days*, 2 vols. (New York: 1835), p. 846.

p. 28   "It needs no prophetic eye . . ." *Report of the Commissioner of Indian Affairs for 1863*, pp. 105–109.

p. 28   "What the white man does . . ." *The War of the Rebellion, 1st ser., vol. 43, pt. 2*, pp. 1150–1151. A compilation of the Official Records of the Union & Confederate Armies, Washington, D.C., 1880–1890.

p. 29   "You are stronger . . ." Worcester, p. 86.

pp. 30–31   "That old murderer . . ." Worcester, p. 90.

pp. 34–35   "I no longer want to live . . ." Worcester, p. 123. Second half of the quote is from Report of the Secretary of the Interior, 42nd Congress, 2nd Session, 1871. Executive Doc. I, vol. 3, serial set 1505. p. 470. Changed from third to first person.

p. 35   "Any coward can kill his enemy . . ." Worcester, p. 125.

p. 35   "Could I not come . . ." Worcester, p. 137.

p. 36   "Almost all of the paying business . . ." Frank Lockwood. *The Apache Indians* (Lincoln: University of Nebraska Press, 1938), p. 177.

p. 37   "As I took his hand . . ." Lockwood, p. 116.

pp. 37, 39, 40   "We were once a large people . . ." General O. O. Howard. *Famous Indian Chiefs I Have Known* (1908; reprint, Lincoln: University of Nebraska Press, 1989), p. 207.

p. 38   "Juh was very large . . ." Eve Ball. *In the Days of Victorio* (Tucson: University of Arizona Press, 1970), p. 125.

p. 38   "An officer of wonderful experience . . ." John Bourke. *On the Border with Crook* (1891; reprint, New York: Time-Life Books, 1980), p. 30.

p. 39   "Cushing was so sure . . . Eve Ball. *Indeh, an Apache Odyssey* (Provo, Utah: Brigham Young University Press, 1982), p. 26.

p. 39   "It was as though every rock . . ." Roberts, p. 60.

p. 39   "Juh wasn't much interested . . ." Ball, *Indeh*, p. 26.

p. 39   "There is an alley . . ." Bourke. *On the Border with Crook*, p. 31.

p. 40   "That I do not know . . ." Lockwood, p. 129.

pp. 40–41   "The howl that went up . . ." Roberts, p. 98.

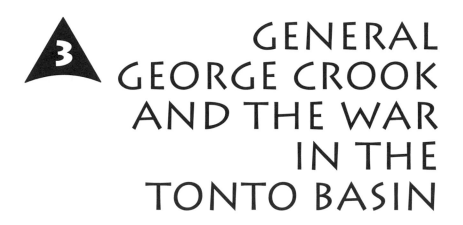

GENERAL GEORGE CROOK AND THE WAR IN THE TONTO BASIN

1871–1874

The peace initiatives for a time seemed to have solved most of the problems with the Apache. Most major groups had settled on reservations that included the core of their traditional territory, including the Mescaleros, Jicarilla and Mimbreno in New Mexico, and the Chiricahuas, Coyotero, and Tonto Apache in Arizona. Most of their leaders advocated peace and realized that they could not long resist the whites. But the peace was to unravel in the course of the next 15 years, because of factors on both sides. On the American side, settlers continued to crowd into the territory and the government proved unable or unwilling to protect the reservations from encroachment. On the Apache side, the leaders who advocated peace proved unable to control young bands of warriors that continued to slip away from the reservation to raid. The chain reaction of settler encroachment, Apache retaliation, and government reaction unraveled the peace first around Prescott and the Verde Valley where early settlement was concentrated.

General George Crook is photographed here on muleback with Apache scouts Dutchy and Alchesay. Crook, the most effective American leader in the war with the Apache, soon realized that the key to success lay in turning the Apache against one another. *(Courtesy Arizona Historical Society, Tucson, Photo AHS 25625)*

Ironically, the onset of President Grant's "peace policy" coincided with the arrival of General Crook in June of 1871, a tough, oddball commander who would prove to be the Apache's most effective and unremitting foe, but also the most compassionate. He rode a mule, wore a pith helmet, and dressed in a canvas uniform. He could outride, out hunt, and out fight most of his soldiers. He displayed a voracious curiosity about the Indians, the terrain, the wildlife, and the plants. His feats of endurance were legendary, his manner gruff, terse, and enigmatic. He typically operated by knowing every detail of organization, interviewing everyone who knew anything about the problem at hand, and then retiring for extended periods to ponder the problem. Then without seeking further counsel, he made his decisions, which he pursued with single-minded ruthlessness. Crook was described as "more Apache than the Apache" by his chief aide in the Apache wars, Captain John Bourke.

Crook often sympathized with the Apache—although he became their most successful enemy. "I think the Apache is painted in darker colors than he deserves and that his villainies arise more from a misconception of facts than from his being worse than other Indians," Crook wrote. "It must be remembered that a large portion of the white population were as barbarous in their modes of warfare as the Apaches themselves; that Arizona was still a refuge for the criminal and lawless men of other states and territories; that war and pillage had been bred into the Apaches, until they were the most savage and intractable Indians in the country; and that large bands of their nation still infested Northern Mexico."

Crook introduced two novel concepts, which became the key to his success. First, he realized that the soldiers must use pack trains to make themselves as mobile as the Apache and pursue campaigns year-round—including winter when the Apache normally retreated into their mountain homes to live on supplies gathered during the summer raiding season. That meant breaking his armies up into many independent commands that could rove freely throughout the countryside. Crook hired the best civilian packers he could find, assembled the best mule strings, and insisted on packs custom designed for each mule. These pack trains made it possible for small detachments to cover a thousand miles in a single expedition. Crook's second innovation was even more crucial. He quickly realized soldiers stood little chance of keeping up with the fleet-footed Apache. Most cavalry companies considered 40 miles a long day's journey. But Apache warriors could cover 40 to 60 miles a day on foot, and up to 80 miles on horseback. When pursued, they simply rode their horses to death, feasted on the bodies, then resupplied themselves at the nearest ranch. Worse yet, few white trackers could follow the faint trail of an Apache war party.

Crook quickly realized he had to turn the Apache against one another by using Indian scouts. Initially, he used scouts from groups long hostile to the Apache—such as the Tohono O'odham. But few other groups could keep up with Apache warriors. Moreover, Tohono O'odham warriors who killed an enemy immediately insisted on returning home to undergo days of sweat baths and purifying ceremonies demanded by their religion for such an act of violence. Crook soon discovered that he could turn one Apache band against another, playing on the deep divisions between bands and between the hard-liners and those who realized that the Apache could not win in the end. Instead of relying on one or two Indian trackers, Crook commissioned whole companies of Apache scouts led by one or two whites and their own war leaders. These scout companies often ranged far ahead of the soldiers and did most of the actual fighting.

PLIGHT OF THE APACHE SCOUTS

Thus began the history of the Apache scouts—warriors who fought other Apache bands in a desperate effort to save their own bands and families. Bourke noted in *On the Border with Crook* that the Apache scouts accounted for every single Indian killed or captured in the Tonto Basin campaign in the early 1870s against the Apache and Yavapai bands of central Arizona, save two—one killed by a cowboy, the other by a reservation Apache. The Yavapai were not Apache but were linguistically related to groups living along the Colorado River. However, the Yavapai had taken up raiding and so were targeted along with the Tonto Apache—who were actually traditional enemies of the Yavapai.

In fact, the division between the Yavapai and the Tonto Apache helped Crook enlist scouts from one group to fight against the other. Crook skillfully exploited the divisions among the Apache. In the end, the scouts shortened the war, which reduced the Apache death toll. The bands that cooperated the soonest also generally wound up with reservations that included more of their homelands, while those who fought longest wound up exiled and imprisoned. But few of the scouts themselves gleaned much benefit from their service to the army.

One poignant incident captures the plight of many scouts. A group of scouts under the direction of Al Sieber pursed a band of renegades for days through the rugged Tonto Basin. They finally cornered the fleeing band in a rugged canyon. The scouts advanced carefully, picking their way through the rocks. Suddenly, a woman called out the name of one of the scouts. The young warrior stood frozen by the sound of his mother's voice. Sieber, crouched behind a rock nearby, heard the call and turned to watch the scout intently. The scout stood immobilized for a moment, then dropped into a crouch and begin to slip away from the line. Sieber shot the scout dead before he had a chance to join his family. Sieber, one of the most successful whites in leading the Apache scouts, noted: "When I tell them I am going to kill them, I do it. And when I tell them I am their friend, they know it." Many officers who worked with the scouts came to admire them. "The longer we knew the Apache scouts, the better we liked them," observed Bourke. "They were wilder and more suspicious than the Pimas and Maricopas, but far more reliable and endowed with a greater amount of courage and daring."

Crook planned an immediate campaign against the warring Apache, traveling thousands of miles back and forth across Arizona and into New Mexico to learn the terrain and train his troops. But just as he prepared to launch his campaign, President Grant's peace policy intervened. Crook waited restlessly for permission to launch his campaign, as first Colyer then General Howard came to make peace and establish the boundaries of the new reservations. Crook believed the peace missions would be failures until the Apache had been soundly defeated militarily. He reasoned that a warrior culture would never voluntarily surrender the one activity that had provided wealth, respect, and glory for generations. Howard's arrangement with Cochise resulted in the establishment of the Chiricahua reservation, and the near cessation of Apache raids on the American side of the border in that region. But in the Tonto Basin and the area around present-day Prescott and the Verde Valley, the Tonto and Yavapai soon found it impossible to live peacefully with the rising flood of settlers.

Army Chief of Scouts Al Sieber was respected and feared by the Apache scouts and played a key role in many of the most important events of the Apache wars. *(Courtesy Arizona Historical Society, Tucson, Photo AHS 1967)*

NOVEMBER 1872: GENERAL CROOK MOUNTS TONTO BASIN CAMPAIGN

A succession of incidents triggered the Tonto Basin campaign. Settlers in the area often attacked isolated Apache bands without warning, applying the frontier philosophy that "the only good Indian is a dead Indian." One prominent rancher took the tactic a step further, offering grain laced with strychnine to one group of nominally friendly Indians. Inevitably, these attacks triggered a response by the Apache, who still considered revenge a moral obligation.

In late 1871, a group of Apache based at a reservation established at Date Creek stopped a stagecoach and killed the passengers. The warriors then decided that they would assassinate Crook, to prevent him from retaliating against them. But friendly Indians warned Crook and foiled the attempt in September of 1871. Crook pursued the fleeing renegades, killing most of them in a succession of engagements.

Crook mounted a major winter offense in 1872. He organized three commands, each consisting of one company of cavalry and about 40 Indian scouts. The commands moved independently through a vast area between the Verde Valley, the present-day Flagstaff area, and the volcanic wilderness that comprised the Superstition Mountains and the Tonto Basin. Each command covered thousands of miles, guided mostly by Apache scouts. They rarely came close enough to actually fight the fleeing warriors. But they often captured their camps, or forced the Indians to flee, leaving their supplies behind.

Crook sketched some of the hardships in his annual report for 1873: "The officers and men worked day and night and with our Indian allies and would crawl upon their hands and knees for long distances over terrible canyons and precipices where the slightest mishap would have resulted in instant death, in order that when daylight came they might attack their enemy and secure the advantage of surprise." This war of attrition doomed the Apache in the end. But two major battles finally served to break the back of the Tonto and Yavapai.

DECEMBER 1872: BATTLE OF THE SALT RIVER CAVE

One major battle came in December 1872, in a remote, inaccessible canyon along the Salt River. The battle was vividly described by Bourke in *On the Border with Crook*. An Apache scout named Nantaje told the soldiers about a deep cave at the base of a great cliff that served as a fortress for a group of Yavapai raiders. Nantaje offered to lead the soldiers to the cave in the darkness, warning that they could easily be wiped out if they were discovered while crossing a faint trail at the base of a looming cliff. Lieutenant William J. Ross and a dozen marksmen went first, following Nantaje along a trail almost too faint to detect. They came suddenly upon the cave at dawn, and opened fire—killing six warriors at the first volley. But the rest of the band retreated into the cave, protected by piles of boulders at the entrance. Reinforced by the rest of the troop, the soldiers called upon the trapped warriors to surrender.

But the warriors merely jeered, turning about and slapping their buttocks in the universal Apache gesture of contempt. The warriors then arched arrows into the air, which did little damage to the soldiers crouched behind their rampart of boulders. The soldiers begin bouncing bullets off the sloping ceiling of the cave, ricocheting bullets down into the cave with deadly effect. The soldiers heard a strange sound coming from the cave. "It was a weird chant, half wail and half exultation—the frenzy of despair and the wild cry for revenge," wrote Bourke in *On the Border with Crook*. "Now the petulant, querulous treble of the [women] kept time with the shuffling feet, and again the deeper growl of the savage bull-dogs, who represented manhood in that cave, was flung back from the cold, pitiless brown of the cliffs," recalled

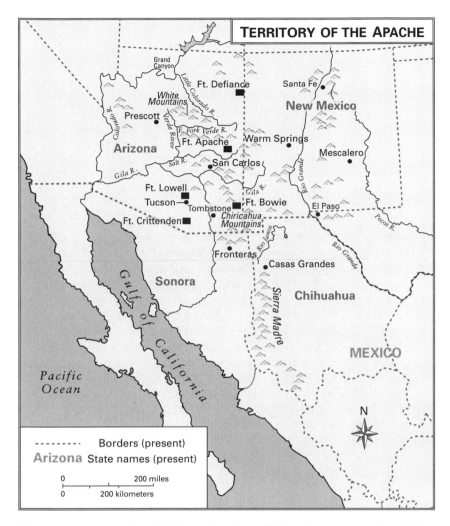

TERRITORY OF THE APACHE

Grand Canyon
Ft. Defiance
Santa Fe
White Mountains
New Mexico
Prescott
Little Colorado R.
E. Fork Verde R.
Ft. Apache
Warm Springs
Arizona
Mescalero
Colorado R.
Verde River
Salt R.
San Carlos
Gila R.
Gila R.
Ft. Lowell
Rio Grande
Tucson
Tombstone
Ft. Bowie
El Paso
Ft. Crittenden
Chiricahua Mountains
Pecos R.
Fronteras
Casas Grandes
Rio Janos
Rio Grande
Gulf of California
Sonora
Chihuahua
Sierra Madre
MEXICO
Pacific Ocean
N

- - - - - - - - Borders (present)
Arizona State names (present)

0   200 miles
0   200 kilometers

This map of Arizona, New Mexico, and northern Mexico shows the area in which the Apache found the Mexicans and Americans during the time period covered in this account.

Bourke. "Look out," cried the Apache scouts, "there goes their death chant, they're going to charge."

Sure enough, a moment later 20 warriors rushed from the cave, "superb-looking fellows all of them," noted Bourke. They charged the double line of soldiers, providing covering fire for another group of warriors trying to slip around the end of the soldiers'

JOHN BOURKE

Captain John Bourke left perhaps the most vivid, articulate, thoughtful, first-person accounts of the Apache wars. He exemplified the best of the professional army—educated, literate, insightful. Raised in a dutiful Irish American family, he enlisted as a teenager to fight the Civil War. He rose rapidly through the ranks, at one point earning the Congressional Medal of Honor for taking command of his company after all of the officers were killed. He remained in the army after that war, finishing West Point, then heading out west for the Indian wars.

He brought extraordinary gifts and a refined intellect to the task. He could read Latin, spoke English and Spanish, and developed a stylish, funny, vivid style of writing. He often found himself in sympathy with his enemies, and disgusted by his allies—including the Indian-hating settlers and the swarm of contractors and speculators who profited from the Indian wars. He also became General Crook's staunchest defender, helping to ensure Crook's place in history despite the political machinations of his superiors. Even more remarkably, Bourke soon developed a lively interest in the native cultures he labored with such energy to destroy. His copious field notes eventually yielded an Apache dictionary and anthropological books about Apache medicine men, the Hopi Snake Dance, and the Lakota (Sioux) Sun Dance. His incessant writing prompted the Apache to call him "Paper Medicine Man."

Bourke left one particularly vivid account of a battle between a troop led by Lieutenant Cushing and a band of Tonto Apache, who had raided a supply train, killing three men. Led by Apache scout Manuel Duran, the soldiers clung to the trail of the raiders for days, following them at last to a mountaintop. The soldiers cautiously surrounded the warriors as they slept.

"One of the old men . . . felt the cold and arose from his couch to stir the embers to a blaze. The light played fitfully upon his sharp features and gaunt form, disclosing every muscle," Bourke wrote in *On the Border with Crook.* "To get some additional fuel, he advanced toward the spot where Cushing crouched awaiting the favorable moment for giving the signal to fire. The savage suspects something, peers ahead a little, and is satisfied that there is danger close by. He turns to escape, crying out that the Americans have come."

Captain John Bourke left compelling first-person accounts of the Apache wars and served as General Crook's chief defender in the historical record. He also became a student of Apache culture and published several anthropological works. *(Courtesy Arizona Historical Society, Tucson, Photo AHS 7812)*

The soldiers opened fire with devastating effect. Roused from their sleep, the warriors quickly formed a defensive line so that the women and children could climb down a cliff at the back of the camp. "They made the best fight they could, but they could do nothing," wrote Bourke. "Manuel saw something curious rushing past him in the gloom. He brought his rifle to shoulder and fired, and, as it turned out, killed two at one shot—a great strong warrior and a little boy of five or six years old whom he had seized and was trying to hurry to a place of safety, perched upon his shoulders. It was a ghastly spectacle, a field of blood won with but slight loss to ourselves," concluded Bourke.

line. However, furious fire drove the warriors back into the cave with heavy losses. One warrior did slip through the first line of soldiers. He rose to jeer at them, not realizing a second line of soldiers crouched behind another line of boulders.

> His chant was never finished; it was at once his song of glory and his death song . . . Twenty carbines were gleaming in the sunlight. The Apache looked into the eyes of his enemies, and in not one did he see the slightest sign of mercy; he tried to say something, what it was we never could tell. "No! No! Solados!" in broken Spanish, was all we could make out before the resounding volley had released another soul from its earthly casket. He was really a handsome warrior; tall, well-proportioned, finely muscled, and with a bold, manly countenance . . . I have never seen a man more thoroughly shot to pieces than was this one.

The Apache in the cave resumed their death chant "with vigor and boldness" and the soldiers resumed bouncing bullets off the roof of the cave. Suddenly, a four-year-old boy ran to the mouth of the cave "and stood, thumb in mouth, looking in speechless wonder and indignation at the belching barrels." Almost immediately, a bullet glanced off his skull, knocking him to the ground. Nantaje sprang to his feet, rushed forward, seized the boy by the arm, and dragged him to safety, drawing cheers from the soldiers who momentarily stopped firing. Then the firing resumed, redoubled in intensity.

"It was exactly like fighting with wild animals in a trap: The Apaches had made up their minds to die if relief did not reach them," recalled Bourke. At this point, another company of soldiers arrived at the top of the cliff, some 400 feet above the cave. Their commander promptly made a harness of suspenders and lowered two men down the cliff face so they could shoot down at the Indians at the entrance to the cave. When they used up their ammunition, they hurled their revolvers in their excitement. "This kind of ammunition was rather too costly, but it suggested a novel method of annihilating the enemy," observed

Bourke. The soldiers rolled boulders off the cliff, which landed with shattering effect at the entrance to the cave. "The noise was frightful; the destruction sickening, since most of the Apaches were crouched behind boulders at the front of the cave to avoid the bullets bouncing off the roof of the cave," recalled Bourke. "No human voice could be heard in such a cyclone of wrath." Nonetheless, through the swirling, choking clouds of dust, the soldiers could see an Apache shaman with a feathered headdress kneeling behind a boulder at the front of the cave, methodically firing then handing the gun back to someone behind him for reloading.

But soon enough, all signs of life in the cave ceased. Soldiers advanced to find a ghastly scene of slaughter. "There were men and women dead or writhing in the agonies of death, and with them several babies, killed by our glancing bullets, or by the storm of rocks and stones that had descended above," wrote Bourke. They found 76 dead, and 35 survivors—half of whom later died. The one surviving warrior had six wounds, and did not live long. They found the shaman, crushed beneath a boulder. They left the bodies where they lay, retreating with their prisoners, lest another band of Apache ambush them on the trail out of the canyon.

MARCH 1873: BATTLE OF TURRET PEAK

One other major battle finally broke the back of the Tonto and Yavapai resistance. The groundwork for the Battle of Turret Peak was laid when a band of Tonto raiders struck scattered settlements around Wickenburg in March of 1873—stealing horses and killing three settlers. Their victims included Gus Swain, a 21-year-old Indian fighter of some note, who once charged through a hail of bullets that riddled his clothing to scalp a Yavapai chief. He later presented the scalp to the editor of the *Prescott Miner*, who proudly nailed it to the front door of the newspaper. The raiders captured Swain and John McDonald, tied them to cactus, and filled them full of arrows. They also captured George Taylor, a miner on a stroll near his house. They bound his hands and feet, then methodically filled his body with arrows—careful not to hit a vital spot prematurely. Friends later found his body bristling with 150 arrows, many broken off as he rolled about in his death throes.

Crook immediately ordered several detachments to scour the surrounding countryside for signs of the raiders. Eventually, a cavalry detachment captured an Apache woman and forced her to lead them to her band. The troopers and scouts approached Turret Mountain in the darkness, creeping up through the brush, and over the rocks, on hands and knees wrapped with rags to muffle any possible sound. They inched to the top of the hill, then opened fire on the sleeping camp. The attack virtually wiped out the Tonto band, without the loss of a single soldier. Surviving accounts offer widely divergent statistics. The official tally includes 33 Indians killed and 13 captured. The *Prescott Miner* reported 47 Indians killed and 7 captured.

In any case, the battle proved decisive. The Yavapai and Tonto surrendered piecemeal in the next few months, lamenting that they could fight the army but not the scouts who could find them in their most secret places so that they couldn't shoot game, light a fire, or linger in one place. One of the last to surrender was Delshay, one of the most determined war leaders. He surrendered several times, repeatedly leaving the reservation again after some incident. General Crook in his autobiography quoted Major George Randall, who accepted Delshay's surrender:

> Delshay commenced crying and said he would do anything he would be ordered to do. He wanted to save his people, as they were starving. He had nothing to ask for but his life. He would accept any terms. He said he had 125 warriors last fall, and if anybody had told him he couldn't whip the world he would have laughed at them, but now he had only 20 left. He said they used to have no difficulty eluding the troops, but now the very rocks had gotten soft, they couldn't put their foot anywhere without leaving an impression we could follow, that they could get no sleep at nights, for should a coyote or a fox start a rock rolling during the night, they

would get up, and dig out, thinking it was we who were
after them.

Initially, the surrendering Tonto and Yavapai bands fared well.
Crook settled them near Camp Verde alongside the Verde River
and put the Indians to work providing hay and firewood for the
fort and planting crops. The Indians labored, hacking miles of
irrigation canals out of the earth with fire-hardened sticks. But the
labor paid off, with successively larger crops in two growing
seasons. Their herds also begin to grow, and it seemed that they
would make a go of it on a reservation established along the river
near the fort. But settlers continued to crowd into the Verde
Valley. Soon, they turned jealous eyes on the productive farmland
of the now peaceful Indians. Meanwhile, Congress shifted respon-
sibility for the Indians from the army to the Department of the
Interior. That opened the door to pressure from contractors and
settlers, who insisted federal officials remove the Indians. Over
Crook's objections, the government agreed.

In February 1875, in the dead of a harsh winter, the government
ordered a small detachment under Lieutenant Eaton to escort
some 1,426 Indians from Camp Verde across 180 miles of snow-
covered peaks, icy, rushing rivers, and hard terrain to the San
Carlos Reservation, a bleak, malaria-ridden lowland selected as
the ideally worthless place to concentrate the defeated Apache
bands from throughout the state. Eaton, his sympathies all with
the Indians, called it "about as ugly a job as was ever laid on the
shoulders of a subaltern in the days of our service in old Arizona."
The government insisted that the procession of mostly women
and children march over the mountains instead of along a wagon
road. One man carried his disabled wife on his back the whole
way. Most of the cavalrymen gave up their horses so that children
could ride. The soldiers did their best to keep the Tonto and the
Yavapai separated, since Crook had often used one band as scouts
against the other—sowing a harvest of deep hatred between the
two groups. At one point, a ball game between children of the rival
bands led to an outbreak of fighting in which five Indians were
killed before the soldiers could break it up. All told, nearly 100

DELSHAY—DEFIANT TO THE END

Delshay's name has mostly been lost to history, an Apache warrior consigned to obscurity because he died too soon and too far from the action later mythologized by pulp novels and clichéd western movies. Born somewhere in the Mazatzal Mountains between 1835 and 1840, Delshay was the most determined, feared war leader of the Tonto Apache, who once held sway over a gigantic swath of central Arizona. Early on, he developed a hatred for Americans. His brother, Rising Sun, was killed for no recorded reason while visiting an army camp. Delshay himself was shot and nearly killed on two different occasions while visiting army posts, for reasons that didn't seem important enough to record.

A bearlike, powerfully built man with a shambling, bowlegged gait, Delshay was a fierce, determined warrior who wandered freely across a rugged wilderness. He habitually moved at a half trot and always wore an ornament in his left ear—avoiding his right ear so it would not interfere with shooting his bow. Delshay proved adept at fighting, surrendering, and recouping his losses on the reservation. In this, he resembled Geronimo, who pursued the same pattern a decade later. On one occasion upon surrendering, Delshay declared: "I don't want to run over the mountains any more. I want to make a big treaty . . . I will make a peace that will last; I will keep my word until the stones melt . . . I will put down a rock to show that when it melts the treaty is to be broken . . . I promise that when a treaty is made the white man or soldiers can turn out all their horses and mules without any one to look after them, and if they are stolen by the Apaches I will cut my throat."

But Delshay could never remain on the reservation for long. Whites continued to intrude on lands set aside for the Tonto and Yavapai, often killing any Indians they found. Delshay also remained deeply suspicious, bolting the reservation on rumors of his imminent arrest and execution. But perhaps most of all, he missed the freedom of a warrior. The fighting whittled down his followers, until he remained in the wilderness with only a handful. Nonetheless, he eluded pursuit by hundreds of soldiers. Finally, General Crook simply put a price on his head and sent Apache bounty hunters out to track him down. Several Apache groups set out after Delshay as well, reasoning that the Americans would take away what little they had left if Delshay continued to raid.

Sometime later, two different groups brought to Crook the head of a warrior to claim the reward. Each seemed to have Delshay's distinctive earring in the left ear. "When I visited the Verde reservation, they would convince me that they had brought in his head. And when I went to San Carlos, they would convince me that they had brought in his head. Being satisfied that both parties were in earnest in their beliefs, and being of the opinion that an extra head was not amiss, I paid both parties," wrote Crook. Ironically, one of the bounty hunters was Desalin, who was himself killed a year later by an Apache policeman—his own brother. It was a strange and bitter revenge for the death of one of the most defiant of Apache warriors.

Indians died or slipped away on the journey. Crook's policy of divide and conquer had produced victory, and reaped its bitter fruit for the Apache and Yavapai.

NOTES

pp. 44–45 "I think the Apache . . ." J.P. Dunn, *Massacres of the Mountains* (N.Y.: 1969) pp. 616–617.

p. 47 "When I tell them . . ." Dan Thrapp. *Conquest of Apacheria* (Norman: University of Oklahama Press, 1967), p. 174.

p. 47 "The longer we knew the Apache Scouts . . ." Bourke, pp. 201–203.

p. 50 "It was a weird half wail . . ." Bourke, pp. 190–201.

p. 54 "His chant was never finished . . ." Bourke, p. 195.

pp. 56–57 "Delshay commenced crying . . ." Thrapp. *Conquest of Apacheria*. p. 142.

p. 57   "about as ugly . . ." William Corbusier. *Verde to San Carlos* (Tucson: University of Arizona Press, 1971), p. 271.

p. 58   "I don't want to . . ." Thrapp. *Conquest of Apacheria.* p. 141.

p. 59   "When I visited . . ." Thrapp. *Conquest of Apacheria.* p. 161.

VICTORIO'S WAR

1875–1880

For a time, in mid-1875, it seemed that perhaps the campaign against the Tonto Apache and Yavapai would end the Apache wars—and convince the other bands to remain on their reservations. The Coyotero, White Mountain, Mescalero, Mimbreno, and Chihenne Apache had all been settled on reservations that included portions of their homelands. The Tonto and Yavapai had been settled on the San Carlos Reservation with the Aravaipa and others—leaving the Verde Valley, the Prescott area, and the Tonto Basin open to white settlement. Even the Chiricahua Mountains had settled on the reservation that Howard had negotiated for them, which included the Dragoon and the Chiricahua Mountains. All of these groups had lost huge tracts of land, but they were generally led by advocates of peace and accommodation. Granted, young warriors still longed to return to raiding, but their leaders mostly held them in check—except on the Chiricahua reservation, where young warriors raided frequently into Mexico.

However, the peace was fleeting—doomed by bureaucracy, greed, and the persistent cultural blindness of the Americans. Almost as soon as President Grant's peace policy succeeded in establishing workable reservations, powerful forces combined to undermine the system.

One of the most important changes was the transfer of General Crook from Arizona to the Great Plains, where the war with the Sioux was raging. Crook had proven himself the Apache's most effective enemy, but also their strongest friend. He treated the Apache with harsh justice, fighting them without hesitation—but treating them with dignity and fair-mindedness once they yielded. He let the Apache on the reservations generally run their own affairs, prevented encroachments on the reservations, and cracked down on corruption. He spoke directly and without embellishment, a trait prized by the Apache, who despised a liar. "It seems likely that if Crook had remained in charge of the Apaches for 10 years, they would have made the adjustment to reservation life and become virtually self-supporting without any major uprisings," concluded historian Donald Worcester, in *The Apaches: Eagles of the Southwest*.

TWO TERRIBLE MISTAKES

Instead, Congress made two terrible mistakes. First, the government decided to reduce costs and open more land to settlement by concentrating as many Apache groups as possible on just one or two reservations. Second, the government transferred authority over the reservations to the Indian Bureau and the Department of the Interior.

Initially, the ideas seemed to have merit—especially when the brash, inexperienced, fearless John P. Clum was appointed as the Indian Agent in charge of the San Carlos Reservation in east-central Arizona—the place chosen to receive Apache bands from throughout the Southwest. Clum was a confident, zealous, energetic, fair-minded man, convinced he could solve the intractable problems that had plagued relations between the Americans and the Apache for two generations. He soon became a fierce advocate for the Indians and a bitter opponent of the army.

Clum insisted that he could run the reservation through the Apache headmen with no help from the army. He established a large Apache police force and court system. He provided jobs and pushed warriors to take up farming and ranching. Somewhat arrogant and self-important, Clum nonetheless made solid friends among the Apache. His initial success was especially remarkable when you consider the character of the San Carlos Reservation, mostly low-lying desert flats along the Gila River. Wretched soils, debilitating heat, barren expanses, and endemic diseases made it

John Clum (center, standing), the San Carlos Indian Agent, is photographed surrounded by some Indians. The scouts called him "Boss with the High Forehead," but the Chiricahua called him "Turkey Gobbler." *(Courtesy Arizona Historical Society, Tucson, Photo AHS 972)*

a thoroughly miserable and unhealthy environment for Clum's experiment in Apache self-government. Apache creation stories suggested that the Creator left the San Carlos area just as terrible, broken, and unusable as he found it, so the Apache could appreciate how nicely he fixed up everything else.

Clum's system might have worked, but it was soon overwhelmed by the effects of the government's concentration policy, and the infighting between the civilian Indian Bureau and the army. Clum's system begin to unravel when the 1,400 feuding Tonto and Yavapai were added to the 1,000 Apache from various bands already at the San Carlos Reservation—including the remnants of Eskiminzin's Aravaipa. But things spun fatally out of control when the government ordered Clum to take his Apache police and round up the Chiricahua led by Cochise's son Taza, which would allow the government to close the Chiricahua reservation promised forever to Cochise by General Howard. Thomas Jeffords had served as Indian Agent there, and he and Cochise had managed to virtually eliminate raiding in the United States by the Chiricahua band. However, the situation on the Chiricahua reservation remained explosive. The reservation lay along the Mexican border, so warriors could easily slip away to raid into Mexico. Moreover, Juh's Nednhi remained in the Sierra Madre, coming and going freely on the Chiricahua reservation. Juh's band included a fierce war leader named Geronimo, whose own band had been virtually wiped out in battles with the Mexicans. Geronimo's wife, mother, and children had all been killed in one attack by Mexican soldiers years earlier, and he had been consumed by an insatiable need for revenge. Juh and Geronimo therefore rode often through the Chiricahua reservation, recruiting warriors for their lethal forays into Mexico.

Moreover, Jeffords found himself locked in an ongoing bureaucratic struggle because of his close relationship with Cochise and his tendency to run the reservation with loose reins. Eventually, these factors convinced the government to shut down the Chiricahua reservation and transfer the seemingly compliant Chiricahua to San Carlos.

Cochise's sons Taza and Naiche and about 325 of their followers reluctantly agreed to the transfer. But Geronimo, Juh, and perhaps 400 others slipped away. Now off the reservation and out of control, the escaped Chiricahua resumed raiding—mostly in Mexico. Many showed up at the Ojo Caliente Reservation, where many had relatives among Victorio's Chihenne. Settlers blamed their raids on Victorio's band. The charges probably had some merit, since young Chihenne warriors often slipped away to join the Chiricahua raiders. In addition, Victorio probably continued to lead his own warriors on raids into Mexico, to augment their scanty rations, and maintain his position of authority in the tribe.

Eventually, the Indian Bureau made another fateful decision and in April of 1877 sent Clum and his Apache police once again into the field—this time to arrest Geronimo, shut down the Ojo Caliente Reservation, and bring Victorio's people to San Carlos. Clum succeeded audaciously on all counts. Clum set a trap for Geronimo, waiting to confront him with a small group of Apache police while a much larger group of Apache police and soldiers waited in hiding. It represented the only time in Geronimo's long career that he was actually captured.

VICTORIO AND LOZEN EMERGE

Victorio ranks as perhaps the most brilliant military strategist on the Apache side in the entire conflict. Quiet, dignified, and fearless, Victorio emerges from the historical record as a ruthless, daring, audacious warrior desperate to find some way to avoid fighting. Throughout his life, he displayed a tenacious reverence for his homeland, and in the end proved that he would rather die than forever leave it. Victorio never matched the diplomacy of Mangas Coloradas, nor the political skills of Cochise, so he could never form alliances that extended much beyond his devoted band of followers. But he proved himself a military genius in guerrilla warfare.

This is the only known photograph of Victorio, the great chief of the Chihenne Apache. Reportedly when this photo was taken Victorio was being held between two guards, accounting for his haunting appearance. *(Courtesy Arizona Historical Society, Tucson, Photo AHS 30371)*

Part of his success apparently stemmed from his relationship with his sister, Lozen—one of the few women to play a leading role as a war leader. Certainly, Apache women played a crucial part in the long war with the Americans. Most knew how to use weapons, and virtually all carried knives. Often, married women accompanied their husbands on raids. Usually, the female relatives of warriors killed on raids were the ones who initiated revenge raids and executed the resulting prisoners. Once the

Americans came, the women and children shared most of the hardships and dangers of the men, since most bands that fled the reservations included women and children.

Apache accounts indicate that Lozen fell in love with a war chief from another tribe, as he wandered through New Mexico seeking some refuge for his people. He continued in his quest, and Lozen resolved never to marry. Instead, she devoted her life, and her great gifts, to helping her brother. She proved adept at fashioning military strategy and reportedly helped her brother formulate his plans. She also showed exceptional abilities as a horse thief, and her name in Apache means "Dexterous Horse Thief." She repeatedly won the admiration of the warriors by slipping alone into soldiers' camps and riding out with their horses. In addition, the Apache say that Lozen had several Powers that proved vital to the survival of her people. She had Power over horses and the Power to cure wounds. Most importantly—she had the ability to locate the position of the enemy. She would stand in a ring of warriors, extend her palms, and turn slowly in a circle—chanting a song that had been taught to her in a vision by White Painted Woman, the protector and mother of the Apache. James Kaywaykla repeated that song to historian Eve Ball:

> In this world, Ussen has Power
> This Power he has granted me
> For the good of my people
> This I see as one from a height
> Sees in every direction;
> This I feel as though I
> Held something in my palms
> Something that tingles.
> This Power is mine to use
> But only for the good of my people.

When she faced the direction from which the enemy was coming, her palms would grow warm. The degree of warmth indicated how close the enemy had come. Apache informants repeatedly asserted that Lozen's Power helped account for her brother's astonishing success in moving freely throughout the

Southwest while pursued by thousands of soldiers. "Power is a mysterious, intangible attribute—difficult to explain even by one possessing it," Ace Daklugie told Ball, who recorded his observations in *Indeh, an Apache Odyssey*. "It was even above courage the most valuable attribute of a chief. Without it, how could he maintain discipline and hold his warriors? You know that Apaches are not easily controlled. Unless they believe their leader has Power, he's out of luck."

Victorio and Lozen tried desperately to follow in the footsteps of Mangas Coloradas and find a way to hold onto the land of their people despite the arrival of the Americans. But the concentration policy that forced them to move to San Carlos signaled the end of that dream in April of 1877. Victorio was initially taken to San Carlos in chains, along with Geronimo's Chiricahua who had taken refuge at the Warm Springs reservation after the government closed the reservation that included the Dragoon and the Chiricahua Mountains. Victorio's band did not remain long at San Carlos. The Chihenne were allotted a barren tract of land along the Gila near Camp Goodwin, the site of an army post that had been abandoned after an epidemic of malaria killed one-quarter of the garrison. They suffered a rising infant and child death rate, but the restrictions on them prevented them from moving away from the area as had been their custom. In addition, the Chihenne soon found themselves fighting with other Apache groups crowded onto the reservation, particularly the Chiricahua. "The Creator did not make San Carlos," James Kaywaykla told historian Eve Ball many years later. "It is older than He . . . He left it as a sample of the way they did jobs before He came along . . . Take stones and ashes and thorns and with some scorpions and rattlesnakes thrown in, dump the outfit on stones, heat the stones red hot, set the United States Army after the Apaches and you have San Carlos."

On September 2, 1877, Victorio led perhaps 300 of his people off the San Carlos Reservation, including 52 warriors. Victorio skillfully eluded the pursuit of the army and the Chiricahua and Coyotero Apache scouts, returning to Ojo Caliente. Victorio spent the next two years trying to convince the Americans to let his band remain at Ojo Caliente. He offered to live on half rations and to maintain the peace himself. On one occasion, seven warriors stole some horses and cattle from Americans near the reservation. Victorio sent Nana after the renegades, who soon captured them. The defiant warriors insisted they were powerful witches, and that they would curse Nana. The implacable Nana freed one boy who had been their prisoner, and then killed the six renegades. Government policy flip-flopped. Several times, the government decided to force them to return to San Carlos—but Victorio inevitably got wind of the plans and vanished. On another occasion, the government opened negotiations with Victorio and agreed to let his band join their allies on the Mescalero reservation. But the translator apparently bungled the translation, and Victorio apparently thought his band would be forced to return to San Carlos. He stood abruptly, and raced from the conference shouting: "Never. I would die first."

A FATAL MISUNDERSTANDING

The Indian Bureau finally decided to settle the troublesome issue by yielding to Victorio and establishing a reservation for the Chihenne at Warm Springs. Unfortunately, as the government blundered haltingly toward the decision that would have prevented problems years earlier—Victorio learned of a warrant for his arrest issued by civilian officials in Grant County for horse theft and murder. Already skittish at the possibility that he would be seized and summarily executed like Mangas Coloradas, Victorio learned in September of 1879 that a local judge, a prosecuting attorney, and several others were crossing the reservation. In fact, it was merely a hunting party. But Victorio decided that they had come to arrest him, and so bolted for the last time from the Mescalero reservation where his people had settled waiting for a government decision.

Victorio, Nana, and at least 40 warriors, moving ahead of several hundred women and children, swooped down on the

Ninth Cavalry's horse herd at Warm Springs—killing the eight guards and stealing the horses they needed to make their escape. The breakout started a string of running battles that would continue for nearly two years, terrorizing the Southwest. Victorio's ranks were sometimes swelled by recruits from the reservations, sometimes numbering more than 100. Victorio's people endured terrible hardships, living on the run among innumerable enemies, fighting with little real hope, and with nothing left to lose. Nonetheless, Victorio rallied his people. "Every struggle, whether won or lost, strengthens us for the next to come," he said. "It is not good for people to have an easy life. They become weak and inefficient when they cease to struggle. Some need a series of defeats before developing the strength and courage to win a victory." Other members of his band recalled the hardship of that fight. "Until I was 10 years old, I did not know that people died except by violence. That is because I was an Apache, a Warm Springs (Chihenne) Apache, whose first vivid memories are of being driven from our reservation near Ojo Caliente with fire and sword," recalled James Kaywaykla.

Many of the soldiers who pursued Victorio relentlessly sympathized with his fight to retain his grip on his homeland. "It is believed by many that Victorio was unjustly dealt with in the first instance by the abrupt removal of his people from Ojo Caliente to San Carlos, and that such a removal if not a breech of faith was a harsh and cruel measure, from which the people of New Mexico reaped bitter consequences," observed General Orlando Willcox, commander of the Department of Arizona. As General Crook commented in 1879: "During the 27 years of my experience with this Indian question, I have never known a band of Indians to make peace with our government and then break it, or leave their reservation, without some ground of complaint; but until their complaints are examined and adjusted, they will constantly give annoyance and trouble."

But the press, the settlers, and the politicians soon raised a panic-stricken howl of protest, outraged that "uncivilized" savages could defy the United States of America, killing with seeming impunity. "We are dreaming of a golden age—a future empire—and fifty dirty, lousy Indians have us in a state of siege," screamed the *Silver City Daily Southwest* in 1880.

But Victorio seemed impossible to catch. Fleeing the reservation, his warriors fought repeated, sharp engagements with the soldiers pursuing them. Typically, Victorio's warriors would select a strong defensive position, wait for the Apache scouts to lead the soldiers along their back trail, then spring their ambush. Repeatedly, the soldiers took cover, and they spent several hours trying to encircle and entrap the warriors—only to find that Victorio had vanished. The soldiers usually lost a few men, Victorio even fewer. In fact, Victorio's fighting force grew initially, augmented mostly by Mescalero warriors who slipped away from their reservation in New Mexico. His fighting force grew gradually, peaking at about 150 warriors.

Victorio fought dozens of engagements, winning every one. He ranged freely across New Mexico, and down into Mexico. At one point, he sent a warrior who spoke Spanish into the Mexican town of Carrizal to gather any potentially useful information. The warrior discovered that the people of Carrizal planned to invite Victorio to a fiesta, ply his warriors with tequila, and then kill them—just as others had done to Mangas Coloradas's band decades before. Instead, Victorio sent several warriors to steal a horse herd from a pasture within sight of the city. Eighteen soldiers and vaqueros set out to recover the herd, but the warriors led them into a carefully prepared ambush in the Candelaria Mountains. Victorio then hid the 18 bodies, and waited. Soon, a force of 35 would-be rescuers rode into the same trap. Victorio's warriors killed 15 of them, before letting the rest escape.

Still, their pursuers hung onto their trail, thanks mostly to the efforts of the Apache scouts working with the soldiers. Detachments of 50 to 100 soldiers, usually with 20 or 40 Apache scouts, crisscrossed the Southwest, harrying Victorio. Often, these detachments covered 1,500 miles in a single expedition, without ever catching sight of Victorio's warriors.

Victorio for a time also joined forces with Geronimo and Juh's Nednhi, who had taken advantage of the chaos caused by Victorio's breakout to resume raiding in the United States from their sanctuary in the Sierra Madre. Ironically, Victorio had long been critical of Geronimo—whose unceasing raids had helped provide the government with the excuse it needed to shut down first the Chiricahua reservation and then Ojo Caliente. For a time, the combined force of Chihenne, Mescalero, and Nednhi seemed unstoppable—led by the two greatest military strategists in Apache history. But Thomas Jeffords soon found his way to Juh's camp and convinced Geronimo and Juh to forsake the warpath and settle again at San Carlos with the rest of the Chiricahua. The defection fatally weakened Victorio's force, allowing the army to concentrate its attention on the Chihenne.

The unceasing pursuit begin to wear down the Chihenne—whose band still consisted mostly of women and children. "The troops were enabled to hold on the trail as long as the Indians left one," noted Lieutenant Thomas Cruse, in *Apache Days and After*. "As the Apache is a temperamental person in spite of his stoicism, this persistent following got on his nerves."

Finally in May of 1880, a group of Apache scouts led by Henry K. Parker surprised Victorio's camp in an isolated canyon near the headwaters of the Palomas River in New Mexico. Parker and about 50 scouts had moved far ahead of the mounted soldiers, who couldn't keep up with the scouts. The scouts caught Victorio in one of his few lapses, encamped in a position in which he could be encircled and trapped. The scouts sprang the trap at dawn, driving Victorio's band into a jumble of rocks. The battle went on all day, and Victorio lost 35—mostly warriors. Parker sent for help, but his message was ignored. The scouts ran out of ammunition after a fierce daylong fight—and had to withdraw. They retreated as Victorio's men followed to harass them. At one point, the scouts were reduced to eating their own horses. Nonetheless, the ambush by the scouts counted as Victorio's only serious defeat in his long running battle with the armies of both the United States and Mexico.

1880: FORTUNE TURNS

Fortune soon turned against the resourceful Victorio. Enraged by the role of the scouts in hunting down his people, Victorio sent his son with a band of warriors back to San Carlos Reservation to make good on his threat to retaliate against the families of the scouts. But the war party mistakenly attacked a Nednhi camp. Pursued by soldiers from the reservation, Victorio's son was killed in a short, fierce battle. Victorio retreated into Mexico but soon had to undertake another raid into the United States to obtain ammunition for his warriors' American-made guns. Growing desperate, Victorio attacked a military supply train that proved to be an ingenious trap. Soldiers hidden in the wagons threw back canvas coverings and opened fire on the attacking warriors.

Victorio retreated once again toward Mexico. As they neared the border, Mescalero war chief Cabrillo challenged Victorio's leadership. By this time, Mescalero warriors composed about half of Victorio's fighting force. Cabrillo insisted that Victorio had lost his war Power, and said he would take his warriors back to the Mescalero reservation. Instead, Victorio killed him in a knife fight for leadership. Victorio then suffered another loss. Just as the Chihenne prepared to cross the Rio Grande into Mexico, a Mescalero woman began to give birth. Lozen tended to the woman and decided to leave the band and escort the woman back to the Mescalero reservation across hundreds of miles bustling with enemy soldiers. She reached the reservation with the woman and her baby safely, but she was not with Victorio as he fled on into Mexico. Victorio met with the other Apache leaders, and eventually decided to head for a low range of hills called Tres Castillos, noting that just beyond that landmark he had cached supplies, including ammunition. He also dispatched Nana, Kaytennae, and several warriors to find ammunition while the rest of the band journeyed to Tres Castillos.

But a Mexican army under Colonel Joaquin Terrazas came across Victorio's trail and followed him to Tres Castillos. The Mexicans attacked at sunset in October of 1880. Those who could, scattered. Victorio rallied the main body of warriors and fought

THE SAGA OF KAYTENNAE: FLYING WITHOUT FEATHERS

The first shots shattered the weary stillness of the Apache camp, jarring James Kaywaykla into sudden awareness of their peril. Kaywaykla's stepfather, Kaytennae, yelled at him to move up the slope toward the prearranged escape route. The boy noted the red headbands on the enemy, and realized that the hated Apache scouts had led the soldiers to their camp. The warriors ran toward the attacking scouts, to cover the retreat of the women and children. Fortunately, Kaytennae, whose name means "flight without feathers" in recognition of his courage, realized that another, larger force of soldiers was closing in from another direction.

Kaytennae immediately rallied two other warriors, and they charged the soldiers, shooting furiously. Kaytennae was the most respected marksman in the band and was believed to have the power to dodge bullets. The soldiers fell back in confusion, leaving some of their mounts, but wounding one of the warriors. Kaytennae quickly captured one of the soldiers' horses and rescued the wounded warrior. Other warriors now joined them, providing a covering fire that enabled the women and children to escape, scattering to regroup at the prearranged rendezvous point miles away.

Kaytennae's remarkable charge was but one incident in a tumultuous life. He charged through the events of the Apache wars, distinguishing himself as a warrior under Victorio, riding with Nana to exact a bloody revenge, and joining forces with Juh and Geronimo. He finally surrendered and settled on a reservation, where he was arrested for allegedly plotting to kill an army officer, subjected to a sham trial, and imprisoned at Alcatraz for 18 months. This exposure to the power of the white civilization converted him into an advocate for peace, and he helped talk Geronimo into surrendering—only to be rewarded with an exile and imprisonment that lasted to the end of his life.

back. Some 350 soldiers and their Tarahumara Indian allies pressed in, driving Victorio and his warriors to a rocky hill, where they fought all night, exhausting their ammunition. The Mexicans finished the remaining warriors the next day. Mexican accounts generally indicate that Victorio was killed by Mauricio Corredor, captain of a force of Tarahumara Indians fighting with the Mexicans. He was eventually rewarded with the chief's beautifully inlaid saddle. Apache accounts indicate that Victorio and his last few warriors killed themselves with their own knives after they ran out of ammunition. Other accounts suggest he may have been captured and executed. Various accounts provided conflicting details of the fight. The report of the Mexican commander indicated that the soldiers counted 78 bodies, including those of Victorio and 62 warriors. The Mexicans took 68 women and children captives, about 15 of them young boys who had not yet taken the training as warriors.

The prisoners huddled together without food or drink until about midday the next morning. Then the order came to separate the 15 boys from the rest. "They take us now to the brush to kill us," said one of the older boys to the rest. "Let us remember that we are Apaches and show them how men can die!" The boys walked away with the soldiers, heads held high. The shots rang out a short time later.

The soldiers marched the rest of the prisoners on into Mexico for sale as slaves. About 30 warriors escaped, most of them out raiding or hunting. Nana and Kaytennae came upon the scene of the battle after the Mexicans left, with a load of captured ammunition. "Too late, too late," said Kaytennae bitterly. "It is not too late so long as one Apache lives," said Nana.

The survivors regrouped, attacked a retreating column of soldiers, and freed one captive. In late 1881, Nana—then at least 75—led one of the most remarkable revenge raids in history. Nana, Lozen, and Kaytennae rode back into the United States with all their surviving warriors—a total of perhaps 15. They enlisted additional Mescalero warriors, bringing the force up to between 50 and 75. Nana's warriors then rode 3,000 miles in six

TZE-GU-JUNI:
A WOMAN OF POWER

One of the survivors of the battle of Tres Castillos was a remarkable woman named Tze-gu-juni (Pretty Mouth). She was thought to have powers, including the ability to escape injury, the gift of healing, and the ability to help bring babies safely into the world. Tze-gu-juni had been struck by lightning, which killed her mother and sister, but only scarred Tze-gu-juni on the head, breast, and leg—proof of the gift of White Painted Woman.

After Tres Castillos, her gift was tested as never before. She was marched with the others deep into Mexico, then sold to a farmer near Mexico City, more than 1,000 miles from her homeland. Tze-gu-juni worked as a slave in a maguey field for at least three years while she and two other women made their plans to escape. Tze-gu-juni stole a knife, wrapped a blanket under her loose-fitting peasant's clothes, and finally gave the signal to slip away just before dark one cold winter night in 1883. They hid by day and traveled by night, living off the land until they killed a cow at a watering hole, eating the meat raw, using the stomach as a water bag, fashioning moccasins from the hide, and covering their tracks with care. They didn't risk lighting a fire for three months, until they killed another cow at a water hole.

One night as Tze-gu-juni slept, a huge mountain lion pounced suddenly on her. The lion sought its death grip on her neck, but her blanket muffled the bite. The lion clawed her shoulders and head as she struggled, leaving deep gouges in her face and nearly ripping her scalp from her head. She plunged a knife repeatedly into the great cat's side, finally finding its heart. Her companions tended to Tze-gu-juni's awful wounds. They tied her scalp to her head with buckskin thongs, rubbed sputum from the dead lion into her wounds, burned the thorns off cactus pads, split them open, and applied them to the wounds. It was weeks before they could continue, but they eventually made it back to the San Carlos Reservation.

Tze-gu-juni went on to play a key role in future events, partly because of her acquired fluency in Spanish, and partly because of her expertise in making tizwin, the mild Apache liquor made from fermented agave (a local plant). She proved a significant factor in stirring up the conflict and discontent that ultimately led to Geronimo's breakout. She fled with Geronimo but was later recaptured and imprisoned again on the San Carlos Reservation, where she became one of Captain John Bourke's key sources of information about Apache culture. He encountered her the first time in a small cell, the night after she'd delivered the baby of one of the women in the jail—using a tin cup to cut the umbilical chord. He called her Francisca—the Spanish name she used in dealing with the whites. She showed him a flint spearhead made of rock that had been struck by lightning. She chipped off pieces of that talisman and ground it up in water to administer to women having difficult births.

Tze-gu-juni survived decades of warfare and later imprisonment in Florida with the Chiricahua and Chihenne, where Geronimo took her as his wife, calling her "the bravest of Apache women," according to historian Eve Ball. She died of unlisted causes at Fort Sill, Oklahoma, sometime after 1894. She is buried in the Fort Sill cemetery beside Geronimo.

weeks—averaging at least 50 miles a day. They fought seven serious engagements with the cavalry, winning every one. They also attacked a dozen towns and ranches and killed 35 to 50 settlers and soldiers and stole hundreds of horses. Thousands of soldiers gave chase, but Nana didn't lose a single warrior. He returned to Mexico virtually unscathed and joined Juh and Geronimo, who had by then left the reservation and returned to their fortress in the Sierra Madre. Nana's determination had to keep them going in the dark days after the death of Victorio. "Now it is for the living to see that our tribe is not exterminated," said Nana to the handful of survivors. "We must live. We must carry on the fight." But the Chihenne had been broken, along with Mescaleros, Aravaipa, White Mountain, Tonto, Yavapai, and all of the others. There remained only the Nednhi and the Chiricahua—about to face their own struggle.

Nana, the lame Chihenne chief who led an amazing raid when at least 75 years old, survived the destruction of Victorio's band and was among the last Apache to surrender. *(Courtesy Arizona Historical Society, Tucson, Photo AHS 25,634)*

NOTES

p. 68   "The Creator . . ." Ball. *Indeh*, p. 50.

p. 70   "Every struggle . . ." Lee Miller. *From the Heart*. (New York: Alfred A. Knopf, Inc., Random House, 1995), p. 260.

p. 70   "Until I was 10 years old . . ." Worcester, p. 220.

p. 70   "It is believed . . . " Worcester, p. 223.

p. 70   "During the 27 years . . ." Dunn, p. 634.

p. 75   "They take us now . . ." Ball. *In the Days of Victorio*, p. 170.

p. 75   "Too late . . ." Ball. *In the Days of Victorio*, p. 101.

p. 77   "Now it is for the living . . . " Ball. *In the Days of Victorio*, p. 102.

DEATH OF A PROPHET

1880–1882

Tired from a night of frenzied ritual dancing, Noche-del-klinne toiled through the misted moonlight up the long slope to the mesa top overlooking Cibicu Creek sometime in 1881. Three followers walked along behind the most famous medicine man of the White Mountain Apache. Even Nana, the seemingly indestructible and irreconcilable war chief of the Chiricahua Apache walked a pace behind this gaunt mystic, who promised his desperate people miracles and redemption. Nana and the surviving Chihenne had stayed with Geronimo and Juh in the Sierra Madre for much of 1879, before they had decided to surrender finally and return to the San Carlos Reservation, where they could be safe. But they yearned still for the free life, and so listened to the Prophet when he promised that the whites would be destroyed and the Apache would once more be free. Just before reaching the crest of the rise, Noche-del-klinne stopped, dropped to his knees, and begin a long chant—a desperate prayer to the dead. The gentle, slightly built, pale-skinned former scout had mesmerized Apache bands across Arizona with a blend of Apache mysticism and resurrection Christianity. His dreamy promises that the dead chiefs would rise and the whites would leave the land to the Apache had inspired hope in the Apache and growing dread among the whites. "Come to us, show yourselves," cried Noche-del-klinne, the great silver peace medal he'd received personally from President Ulysses S. Grant for his service as a scout dangling about his neck. The predawn mists gathered, swirled, and took ghostly form. "There appeared to us three of those great ones," recalled one of the witnesses later. The forms appeared to be Cochise, Victorio, and Mangas Coloradas. "They were like shadows at first, but we saw them rise out of the ground, very slowly, and coming no further than the knees. All about them they looked." The ghostly chiefs then asked: "Why do you call us? Why do you disturb us? We do not wish to come back. The buffalo are gone. White people are everywhere in the land that was ours. We do not wish to come back." The shaken listeners replied: "But tell us what we must do!" The shades begin to sink once more into the ground saying: "Live at peace with the white men and let us rest."

The moment convinced Nana that Noche-del-klinne did indeed have the power he claimed. And although the message of the dead chiefs seemed clear enough, it set in motion a terrible chain of events.

A TURNING POINT

The strength of this Apache religious movement provided one of the fatal turning points that punctuated the long, bitter struggle between the Apache and the whites. It resembles the Ghost Dance that originated among the Paiute in Nevada in 1870 and again among the Paiute and Sioux in the 1890s. In Arizona in 1881, it came just when it seemed the war with the Apache had ended. General Crook had crushed the Tonto and Yavapai, demonstrating the value of scouts and attrition in breaking down the resistance of these peerless guerrilla warriors. The long war with Victorio had demonstrated to most of the Indians the futility of open resistance with bands that included women and children. What chance did any Apache have of living the old, free life if the brilliant tactician and spiritually powerful Victorio could not elude destruction even in the recesses of Mexico? That's why in the wake of Victorio's death in 1880, such redoubtable warriors as

Geronimo, Nana, and Juh slipped quietly back onto the San Carlos or White Mountain reservations, donned their metal identification tags, and lined up for rations. The army's policy seemed triumphant, having concentrated most of the Apache on the San Carlos Reservation, with other bands settled on the Mescalero reservation in New Mexico or the White Mountain reservation in Arizona. Even the most warlike chiefs seemed reduced to a sullen, wary acceptance.

Then came the Prophet, and his promise that the whites would leave and the Apache would regain their lands. The resulting movement raised the specter the army most feared—not the ghosts of dead chiefs—but the unification of feuding Apache bands. The whites had skillfully utilized the divisions among Apache bands. But whites feared that Noche-del-klinne's unifying philosophy threatened a massive revolt. The Apache could still muster thousands of warriors if the rival bands acted in concert. Warriors came from all over to gather for the days-long sessions of singing and dancing at Cibicu, Noche-del-klinne's base camp on the White Mountain reservation in eastern Arizona.

However, surviving Apache accounts suggest that the whites had once again completely misunderstood their culture and intentions. In fact, the Prophet had actually convinced warriors like Geronimo, Juh, and Nana to remain at peace and leave the whites to Ussen, the creator and guardian of Apache religion. "Of all the encounters Apaches had with their enemies, I believe that Cibicu is least understood by white people," Ace Daklugie told historian Eve Ball. "The Apache Medicine Man used the ghost dance to remind us that Ussen had promised to rid the country of our enemies in His own way and at His own time. Geronimo told me shortly before he died that he never understood why he and Juh could have been so easily influenced by that Medicine Man; but he had convinced them that the Apaches should leave revenge to Ussen."

Noche-del-klinne seemed an unlikely figure to trigger such events. About 5' 5" tall and weighing less than 125 pounds, the wispy, aesthetic, soft-spoken Coyotero Apache first surfaces in historic accounts as an enlisted Apache scout in the 1870s. Noche-del-klinne joined a group of scouts who journeyed to Washington to receive silver peace medals from President Grant, then he attended a government school in Santa Fe. He later returned to his own people in the White Mountains of Arizona, gradually developing a reputation as a healer and holy man. Soon after his return to Arizona, he became known as the Prophet and begin holding ceremonies that mingled traditional Apache beliefs with the Christian notion of resurrection, casting the greatest chiefs of the recent past in the role of the redeemers.

The army gradually grew alarmed. Lieutenant Thomas Cruse, who commanded a company of Apache scouts based at Fort Apache, attended one dance in which people moved in a great circle for hours, singing, chanting, and crying out until they dropped from exhaustion. Cruse reported his amazement at "the unusual mixture of his audience, which included Apaches who had been proscribed as murderers, horse thieves, women stealers; all there mingling with the better element of the tribes who only a short time before had been trying to locate and exterminate these same renegades . . . All seemed under the influence of some strange superstition that lifted them out of themselves and the affairs of this world."

AUGUST 30, 1881: BATTLE OF CIBICU

San Carlos Reservation Indian Agent Joseph Tiffany decided the new religion was a serious threat and sent Apache police to arrest the Prophet, but they returned unarmed and sullen. Tiffany then appealed to the army to "arrest or kill or both" the increasingly influential medicine man. On August 28, 1881, Fort Apache Commander Colonel E. A. Carr reluctantly mounted an expedition, assembling 117 men, including 23 White Mountain Apache scouts, 79 soldiers, six officers, various guides and civilian employees, and his own 15-year-old son. The uneasy company of soldiers and scouts covered the roughly 45 miles to the Prophet's camp on Cibicu Creek in two days. On August 30 the soldiers found the prophet at his wickiup, a brush shelter, eating his supper while reclining on a pile of Navajo blankets, surrounded by perhaps 20 wary, armed warriors.

After some discussion, the Prophet agreed to return with the troops. Colonel Carr placed Noche-del-klinne in the custody of Sergeant John F. MacDonald, ordering the sergeant to shoot the Prophet if he made any attempt to escape or if his followers tried to rescue him. The Prophet only smiled. "No one will try to free me," he said softly. Colonel Carr then turned and left with the bulk of the soldiers, leaving the 23 scouts and 33 soldiers to bring along Noche-del-klinne as soon as he gathered up his things. Carr later drew a censure for dividing his forces at such a sensitive moment. The Prophet sent his son to get his horse, then sat down calmly and resumed his supper. Growing uneasy, Cruse eventually ordered Noche-del-klinne to leave. A soldier pulled the Prophet roughly to his feet. "There was a rustling among that crowd of watching Indians that reminded me of the buzzing of a rattlesnake aroused," Cruse recalled in *Apache Days and After*, where he recorded the dialogue used in this account. Cruse bluffed his way through, ordering Noche-del-klinne to mount up and moving off through the growing crowd of Indians.

Meanwhile, Colonel Carr and Captain Edmund Hentig had selected a defensible campsite on the other side of the creek. They congratulated one another on their unexpectedly easy success. "I was rather ashamed of myself to come out with all of this force to arrest one poor little Indian,"* Carr confided to Hentig. Cruse, the scouts, and the Prophet rode into camp a short while later, placing the Prophet in a sort of corral made of pack saddles. "It looked pretty scaly for a while as we came along," Lieutenant Cruse told the colonel. "Those Indians . . ." The colonel interrupted heatedly: "What are you talking about? You're always using words I don't understand. Scaly! Scaly! Now what does that mean?" Cruse explained: "Well, the Indians kept pouring into the trail of every

---

*Soldier's dialogue in this section came from a primary account, recalled after the events described.

little side canyon. They were all stripped and painted for fighting. It looked like an attack at any minute." Carr seemed puzzled: "Indians, what Indians?"

Cruse gestured towards the creek where a large body of mounted warriors had now come into view. "Keep those Indians out of the camp," Carr ordered. Captain Hentig and an aide walked quickly toward the ford, gesturing vigorously and calling in Apache, "Ucashay. Ucashay (go away)!" Dandy Jim, one of the 23 Apache scouts who had accompanied the soldiers, confronted Hentig, who let him pass through into the army camp. That moment later figured in the trial of the Apache scouts who allegedly fired on the soldiers. The captain then turned to drive off the warriors, who were apparently led by a minor chief and former scout named Sanchez.

Abruptly, someone opened fire, touching a spark to the explosive tension that had been building on all sides all day. The unarmed Hentig and his aide dropped immediately, riddled with bullets. Sometimes confusing and contradictory testimony at the later trial suggested that all of the army's Apache scouts begin firing on the troops, except for Sergeant Mose who ran to Cruse and pleaded for protection from the white troops. The scouts had tried throughout the expedition to protect the Prophet and prevent the outbreak of violence, but now they were forced to chose between their oath to the army and their loyalty to the sense of Apache unity the Prophet had inspired.

An Apache version of the event left by Mike Burns, a Yavapai orphan raised by a white cavalry officer, suggests that Noche-del-klinne's wife pleaded with him to flee. "But when his wife tried to go away over the hills to where the rest had gone, he told her to go alone; that there was no use for him to go anywhere after there had been so much killing on his account, as they would kill him no matter where he went and it was just as well for him to meet his fate where he was."

However, army accounts indicate the Prophet called out to his people to fight, saying he would come to life again if killed by the soldiers. Sergeant MacDonald drew his gun to execute the

THE DEATH OF DEAD SHOT

Three Apaches scouts paid the ultimate penalty for divided loyalties. Dead Shot, Dandy Jim, and Skippy (Skitashe) had all served the U.S. Army loyally for years, until the arrest and execution of the Prophet in 1881 tested their loyalty too far. Dead Shot was popular with the soldiers and nearly legendary for his aim. Sergeant Will Barnes recalled fondly many hunting expeditions with Dead Shot, including one pursuit of a wounded grizzly bear. The pair of hunters tracked the blood trail to a dark cavern in the side of a cliff 300 feet above the valley floor and were discussing how they might force the bear out of its lair when they were terrified by a blood-curdling scream from just behind. They whirled, only to find themselves undone by a mule terrified by the smell of bear. Dead Shot laughed uproariously at his own expense for weeks after that.

But he was judged to be one of six "ring leaders" among the mutinous Apache scouts put on trial, based on vague, sometimes contradictory testimony. Later historians have concluded that although they had clearly deserted, the evidence singling them out for execution in the affair was never convincing. Initially, the army considered a mass hanging of all 17 remaining scouts who had deserted, but eventually staged a trail for just six supposed leaders. Three received death sentences, and two were sentenced to life imprisonment. Dead Shot was in his forties, with a wife and two children. The other two were in their early twenties. As scouts, they had served as a band, subject to their own rules and regulations. They had only a vague sense that they were considered soldiers—subject to the army's harsh code.

Fearful of another outbreak, hundreds of soldiers guarded the parade grounds and the gallows at Camp Grant on March 3, 1882, where a party atmosphere had developed among the delighted spectators. The headline on the story for the *Arizona Star* declared "By the Rope Process Dandy Jim, Dead Shot, and Skippy Become Good Indians,"—referring to the already common saying that "the only good Indian is a dead Indian."

The three doomed warriors watched the construction of the gallows from their jail cell. Dandy Jim refused to eat, but

Dead Shot and Skippy laughed and joked, pantomiming their own jerking and dangling at the end of the rope. "They have no fears of the hereafter and say their hands are clean, meaning innocence, and if nothing can be done for them in this life they are prepared to die," wrote the *Star* reporter. "They mounted the scaffold laughing and showed no signs of fear; said they were happy and would soon meet their friends." Skippy, however, had to be assisted to the noose. Here he said plaintively to the sergeant who steadied him: "Commandanta give Indian clean clothes one day; hang him next day; what for?"

Sixty miles away at San Carlos, Dead Shot's wife hung herself from a tree—a rare suicide among the Apache. "Because she loved her husband very much she wished to go through eternity with him, even though it might have meant a deformed neck," the son of Juh later told historian Eve Ball. Sergeant Will Barnes adopted Dead Shot's two young sons, keeping them on as cowboys when he left the service and started a ranch. They later returned to the San Carlos Reservation, and years later Barnes encountered Dead Shot's grandson. He was a sergeant in the U.S. Army.

Prophet, but Noche-del-klinne's wife covered him with her body, wailing a death chant. The sergeant aimed to avoid hitting the woman and shot Noche-del-klinne. However, MacDonald was felled almost immediately with a bullet to the leg.

In moments, everyone was firing. Hundreds of warriors poured a "murderous" fire into the camp. Carr rallied his troops, issuing orders and firing rapidly "as cool and calm as if he were in his own parlor," noted Cruse. Suddenly, Noche-del-klinne's son galloped into the middle of the fighting, to rescue his father. The soldier's guns thundered and the young warrior plunged from his saddle. His mother rose from her husband's bleeding body and with a terrible cry ran to Captain Hentig's saddle, pulling out a pistol. She was riddled with bullets before she could squeeze the trigger.

Noche-del-klinne begin crawling away. "Why, he's not dead," cried a trooper, who rushed to the wounded Prophet, placed his

Two Apache scouts in chains await hanging for their actions at Cibicu. The scouts who turned on the soldiers during the bungled attempt to arrest an Apache religious leader represented the only such mutiny in the long service of the Apache scouts. *(Courtesy Arizona Historical Society, Tucson, Photo AHS 4593)*

gun against his head, and pulled the trigger. Even that somehow failed to kill the Prophet. Apache accounts suggest that the Prophet was protected from bullets by the magical properties of his shirt. But it's also possible that the trooper's gun misfired. In any case, Noche-del-klinne slumped unconscious but soon revived and begin crawling away again, only to be shot a third time. That still didn't finish him. As he renewed his effort to escape, Sergeant John "Give-a-Damn" Smith crushed his skull with an ax. The sergeant then removed the Prophet's blood-slick medal inscribed: "On Earth Peace, Good Will Toward Men."

A charge by the troops drove the largely disorganized Indians back 300 yards, and the soldiers hunkered down behind cover under long-range sniper fire until nightfall. They slipped away during the night, avoiding an ambush staged by the still disorganized Apache. A total of eight soldiers died, along with an estimated 18 Indians and six scouts. Initially, it seemed the army had crushed Apache resistance. The army sent massive reinforcements to Fort Apache. Many of the chiefs and warriors identified as ringleaders surrendered, although some of those escaped and took refuge with other bands. The army staged a court martial of six scouts alleged to be the ring leaders and then hung Dandy Jim, Dead Shot, and Skippy based on sometimes contradictory or vague testimony. The three scouts met their fate with Apache stoicism, although some of the officers who knew them best lamented their fate, questioning the reliability of the evidence and, although this was the only mutiny of U.S. Army Apache scouts in the field, they also questioned the wisdom of having used the scouts to arrest the Prophet in the face of the resistance of their own friends and family members.

JULY 1882: BATTLE OF BIG DRY WASH

The army also scored one of its few successes in a conventional battle in the aftermath of the events at Cibicu. Several of the Apache army scouts who turned on the soldiers to protect the

Prophet at Cibicu fled to a White Mountain Apache band led by Nantiotish. In July of 1882, a fight broke out between Nantiotish's band and a group of Indian policemen on the San Carlos Reservation—killing eight. Details remain unclear, but the Indian policemen might have been seeking the rebellious scouts who deserted at Cibicu. As a result, a band of perhaps 50 to 70 warriors fled the reservation. They headed for the Tonto Basin and the Salt River, killing anyone in their path.

Three separate cavalry columns, each led by Apache scouts, closed in on the fleeing renegades. In a bit of bad luck for the Indians, the two troops that closed in on them first were both mounted on white horses. Confusion caused by this coincidence was to prove the Apache's undoing. No accounts of the battle have survived on the Apache side. But it appears Nantiotish badly miscalculated, and so violated the cardinal rule of Apache strategy—never give prolonged battle to an equal or superior force.

> This was the only effective concentration of troops ever made against the Apache; and had the Apache been led by such captains as Victorio, Cochise, Mangas Colorado, Nana, or even Geronimo, the concentration would not have been effective. Such a leader would have known the number of troops near him and the Indians would not have stopped to give battle. They would have scattered in the mountains like quail when the hawk dives. But their leader . . . lacked experience, or was not "gifted with the capacity of taking infinite pains." He made a mistake that was fatal to him and to nearly all of his men,

noted Lieutenant Britton Davis, in *The Truth About Geronimo*.

Aware of only one of the three pursuing columns, commanded by Captain Adna Chaffee, Nantiotish crossed the Tonto Basin and headed up a dramatic gash of a canyon toward the forested high country on top of the Mogollon Rim. Egged on perhaps by the renegade scouts who'd once served under the command of Cruse and Al Sieber, Nantiotish selected what seemed to be the perfect spot for an ambush, a canyon 700 feet wide and 1,000 feet deep variously called Chevelon Fork, Canyon Diablo, or Big Dry Wash. The gorge could only be crossed by descending one steep trail then toiling up a trail on the other side. Nantiotish crossed the gorge, then directed his warriors to construct ingeniously concealed fortifications on the other side. His warriors had been keeping track of a single troop of pursuing soldiers, all mounted on white horses—a troop that the Apache comfortably outnumbered. The Apache had probably also spotted the advanced riders of the second troop of soldiers mounted on white horses that followed, but mistook them for stragglers from the first group. Nantiotish thought that if he could catch his pursuers in the open on the trail leading down into the gorge he could all but wipe them out.

But he'd badly miscalculated. First, the army's Apache scouts knew exactly where Nantiotish's band had crossed the canyon, and so spotted the carefully prepared ambush. Second, the soldiers Nantiotish had been watching so intently were joined by a much larger group of soldiers the night before the battle. This gave the army officers time to plan, one of the few times in the 40-year history of the Apache wars in which the army controlled the timing, pace, and unfolding of the battle.

"Nantiotish made several errors of generalship," observed Lieutenant Thomas Cruse, in *Apache Days and After*. "He had watched Chaffee and Sieber all afternoon of the preceding day, counted the soldiers and Indians, and felt confident that his 70-odd renegades could easily wipe them out at Chevelon Fork. Converse's white horses had been taken for Chaffee's. He still had no idea that our force from [Fort] Apache was joined to the little force he had counted—and discounted."

The next morning, the leading cavalry troop advanced to the rim of the canyon, dismounted, and opened up on the concealed Indians—all the while giving the impression that they were considering the vulnerable descent into the canyon on which Nantiotish's trap had been based. But while the soldiers and the Indians exchanged fire across the canyon, two more groups of soldiers set out to close the trap. One troop worked its way to the west along the canyon edge, a second troop pursued the same strategy to the east.

Cruse's troop had just gained the opposite rim in its flanking movement to the east when they ran headlong into a group of warriors who had evidently set out to outflank the small group of soldiers they thought they had pinned down on the opposite side of the gorge. "The flanking party was moving almost carelessly, expecting to scramble easily across the canyon and take Chaffee from the rear," wrote Cruse, whose firsthand account written after the battle provided the dialogue used in this retelling. The warriors fell back in confusion, reaching the main camp just as the jaws of the trap slammed shut. Realizing his mistake, Nantiotish led a rush to the horses, only to discover that another group of soldiers had already come up behind and seized their mounts. The battle now turned into a furious exchange, with soldiers closing in from three sides—trapping Nantiotish's band on top of the cliff.

Bullets found their deadly mark on both sides. One officer renowned for his marksmanship crowded to the front line as the soldiers moved from tree to tree, growing frustrated as his misses mounted. At last, a bullet drove home, and a warrior twisted to the ground. "Got him! I got him!" shouted the lieutenant, half rising from behind cover in his excitement. He was immediately felled by a bullet that shattered his arm, glanced off a rib, punctured a lung, and lodged under the muscles of his back.

The two sides taunted one another as the battle settled into a deadly killing spree. Several of the renegade army scouts found themselves facing Cruse and the other white soldiers who had commanded them before Cibicu. One of those soldiers was Sergeant Conn, a tough, slender Boston Irishman with a thick brogue and 20 years in the service who had been the one to distribute rations. The scouts called him "Coche Sergeant," or "Hog Sergeant," a name that infuriated him. The two sides shouted back and forth, until one warrior who could speak English shouted: "Coward! Hog Sergeant! Come here and I will kill you!" Conn screamed something in reply, and the hidden warrior aimed at the sound of his voice. "Conn went down for the count in the midst of a thrilling repartee," wrote Davis. The bullet hit Conn in the throat, pushing aside the jugular vein, grazing the spine, and leaving a hole the size of a silver dollar in the back of his throat. Amazingly, Conn survived the injury. "I heard the Cap'n say I was kilt. But I knew I was not. I was only spa-a-achless!" Conn explained later.

Cruse, Sieber, and their men worked their way forward toward the trapped Indians, Sieber repeatedly picking off warriors careless of their cover. "I saw him kill three hostiles as they were creeping to the edge of the canyon to drop over [and escape]. He would say 'There he goes!' then bang would go his rifle. The Indian that I had never seen, strain my eyes as I might, would throw up his arms as if trying to seize some support, then under the impetus of his rush, plunge forward on his head and roll over several times. One, shot near the brink, plunged clear over and it seemed to me kept falling for ten minutes."

Cruse then resolved to rush the Indian lines, in hopes of gaining the shelter of an arroyo right at the edge of the Indian encampment. It was by then dusk, and Cruse feared the Indians would escape in the night if the soldiers didn't finish them. "I'm going to that camp," Cruse told Sieber. "No. Don't you do it, Lieutenant! Don't you do it!" Sieber objected. "There's lots of Indians over there and they'll get you, sure!" But Cruse shrugged aside Sieber's warning, and charged forward.

As Cruse later related: "With me were Sergeants Horan and Martin and seven or eight other old-timers. They were not worried in the least by a hot fight, and we were going slap-bang when a hostile appeared not two yards away, leveling his gun directly at me. It seemed impossible for him to miss at that point-blank range, so I raised my own gun and stiffened to take the shock of his bullet. But he was nervous and jerked just enough as he pulled the trigger to send the bullet past me. A young Scotchman named McLellan was just to my left and slightly in the rear. The bullet hit him, and he dropped. I shot the Indian and threw myself to the ground." Cruse dragged the fallen soldier back toward the line, narrowly escaping death once again from a volley unleashed by another line of soldiers. "They did not realize that I was in their direct line of fire two hundred yards away. The air fairly burned with bullets. I was facing the line, and bits of gravel and shreds of bullets stung my face and set it bleeding. I was certain that I had been hit and it was only a matter of moments until I would collapse." Cruse got the soldier back to their lines, but the man "died quietly" an hour later.

The remnants of Nantiotish's band escaped in the darkness—although Nantiotish himself lay dead on the field. The unburied bodies of the Indians marked the spot for years to come, especially the bones of wounded warriors who had crawled away to die in nearby limestone caves. Soldiers counted the bodies of 21 warriors on the field. Only 10 or 15 remained alive; they filtered back onto the reservation and joined other bands. Many of the small, tight-knit but loosely organized Apache bands disappeared in this manner—their losses eventually obliterating the extended family groupings by which Apache society had been organized.

BATTLE'S AFTERMATH

Davis provided a moving epilogue to the battle, in relating the fate of an 18-year-old Apache woman who survived the battle, clutching her infant. Soldiers returned to the Indian encampment at daylight, only to be met by gunfire from behind a small pile of rocks. The soldiers returned fire, and the hidden Apache fell silent. The soldiers crept up on the position, to discover a woman with an empty rifle, a bullet-shattered leg, and a baby. The woman pulled a knife out of her belt and fought furiously as the soldiers grabbed her. She then lapsed into a stoic, uncomplaining silence. The soldiers carried her in a stretcher down the steep gorge and up the other side, jostling her badly wounded leg unmercifully. She uttered not a sound. That evening, a freezing hailstorm hit the camp, and the woman sat in the open, bent over her baby, uncomplaining. The next day the surgeon concluded that infection had set in to her shattered leg, and so he amputated. By then, the

Naiche was the son of Cochise and the last chief of the free Chiricahua.
Naiche never enjoyed the authority of his father. Although he fought nearly to
the end, he remained in Geronimo's shadow.   *(Courtesy Arizona Historical
Society, Tucson, Photo AHS 30,385)*

LIEUTENANT BRITTEN DAVIS

Some of the Apache's greatest sympathizers were among their most effective enemies. The literate, cultured, mostly West Point–educated officer corps that formed the social aristocracy of the frontier army included some remarkable men, who developed a surprising admiration and sympathy for their adversaries. Lieutenant Britton Davis was one of those officers, and his firsthand account *The Truth About Geronimo*, helped shape all subsequent histories. On one occasion, he exerted his considerable ingenuity to save Geronimo from the hangman's noose.

The incident took place some months after Geronimo had met with General George Crook deep within Mexico and agreed to surrender in May of 1882—after he had time to gather up his scattered warriors and their families. Several months later, Davis met Geronimo at the border to escort him safely to the San Carlos Reservation. But Davis was dismayed to discover that Geronimo's warriors were driving along a herd of cattle stolen from Mexican ranches. Davis hurried Geronimo along as quickly as possible. But then the worst happened: A marshall and a customs inspector rode up to the strange column. The marshall promptly deputized the lieutenant, produced a warrant for Geronimo's arrest, and demanded that the army hand over the stolen cattle. This was exactly the situation Lieutenant Davis was supposed to avoid, since an arrest of Geronimo while in army custody would trigger yet another reservation outbreak.

Fortunately, Davis's good friend Colonel Bo Blake arrived at this critical juncture. The two officers quickly came up with a plan: Blake would order Davis to remain in place under the marshall's orders, but the colonel would leave during the night with Geronimo and his herd. "The plan looked simple. So does flying," observed Davis.

That night, Davis plied the marshall and the customs man with good Scotch whisky, encouraging them to drink themselves into a stupor. Then he convinced Geronimo to take his herd and steal away in the night. Initially, it seemed Geronimo would explode in anger and violence at the prospect of being arrested. But then Davis suggested that it would be a great trick for Geronimo to sneak his herd out from under their noses, which appealed to Geronimo's dark sense of humor. The Indians and several hundred cattle disappeared in the night with scarcely a sound. The astonished marshall awoke the next morning, climbed to the roof of the little building in which he'd spent the night, and scanned the empty plains to the distant horizon. Straight-faced, Davis placed himself under the marshall's orders and asked what he should do. "You can go to hell as far as I'm concerned, and I wish you a happy journey" concluded the disgusted lawman. "It was a mighty slick trick, lieutenant, but I never would have believed it possible if I had not seen it."

soldiers had used all of their anesthetic, and even all of their whisky, on their own wounded.

Cruse had intended to watch the operation, thinking he might have to perform the service on one of his own men sometime in the wilderness. "But when I caught a glance from that young woman's eyes as she watched the doctors getting ready, I suddenly decided to get my surgical training some other way," Cruse recalled. There was nothing to deaden the pain, yet she stood it without a murmur. She survived the operation, and the trip back to the reservation, and Davis notes that he saw her years later moving adroitly on her crutch. Unfortunately for history, neither this courageous survivor nor any other participants on the Apache side left an account of this battle.

Seemingly, the battles at Cibicu and Big Dry Wash had crushed Apache resistance. The Prophet's unifying ideology had proved futile against the soldiers' bullets, and the army had proved once again that the Apache stood little chance in a full-scale battle. And yet, this application of direct and brutal force once again failed to end the warfare that had plagued the Southwest for decades. Rather, the attack at Cibicu, the executions of the scouts, the set piece battle at Big Dry Wash had merely convinced the final Apache war leaders that they could not survive on the reservation and could not prevail in open battle.

This set the stage for the final, most famous chapter in the long struggle against this warrior culture. In September of 1881, Geronimo, Juh, Lozen, Natche, and others fled the reservation. The Prophet's reliance on dead chiefs and Ussen's revenge had collapsed in blood and turmoil. The Chiricahua knew only two choices remained: They could submit to humiliation, starvation, and slow death on the reservation or opt for a few more years of freedom and a warrior's death, according to the later accounts by Geronimo and others like Juh's son Ace Daklugie. So they called themselves Indeh—the Dead—and exacted a terrible toll in their long, final defiance of the inevitable. They abandoned any thought of open battles with soldiers and resolved instead to teach the increasingly numerous, scattered, and mostly unprotected white settlers the full meaning of the Apache's rigid code of revenge. All this grew out of the misunderstanding of the teachings of an Apache spiritual leader who nearly convinced Geronimo, Juh, and Nana to lay down their arms and trust in Ussen's intervention. As Captain John Bourke concluded: "There was a coincidence of sentiment among all the people whose opinion was worthy of consideration that blame did not rest with the Indians. No one had heard the Apache's story, and no one seemed to care whether they had a story or not."

NOTES

p. 81   "There appeared to us . . ." Worcester [The dialogue comes from an account by Lieutenant Thomas Cruse who got it from an Apache who was present], p. 239.

p. 82   "Of all the encounters . . ." Ball. *Indeh*, p. 52.

p. 83   "the unusual mixture . . ." Thomas Cruse. *Apache Days and After* (Lincoln: University of Nebraska, 1941), p. 96.

p. 84   "It looked pretty scaly . . ." Cruse, p. 108.

p. 85   "But when his wife . . ." Ball. *Indeh*, p. 54.

p. 86   "By the Rope Process . . ." Roberts, p. 200.

p. 87   "Because she loved her husband . . ." Ball. *Indeh*, p. 55.

p. 90   "This was the only effective . . ." Davis, p. 13.

p. 91   "Nantiotish made several errors . . ." Cruse, p. 164.

p. 92   "Got him, I've got him . . ." Cruse, p. 166.

pp. 92–93 "Conn went down . . ." Britton Davis. *The Truth About Geronimo* (Lincoln: University of Nebraska Press, 1929; reprint), p. 22.

p. 93   "I saw him kill . . ." Davis, p. 22.

p. 97   "But when I caught . . ." Davis, p. 26.

p. 98   "There was a coincidence . . ." Ball. *Indeh,* p. 55.

THE LAST
OF THE
FREE LIFE

1882–1883

Cibicu and its bloody after-math set in motion the final struggle in the Apache's long fight to save their land and their culture. This last chapter would be dominated by Geronimo—daring, courageous, cruel, indomitable, treacherous. He became one of the most famous of all Native Americans, as a result of his audacity and persistence. He also managed to reap lavish news coverage—perhaps simply because he was the last and continued fighting when most of the country had succumbed to the plow and the barbed-wire fence. Ironically, Geronimo never led great Apache armies in battle and never served as the chief of a band. Geronimo was a shaman and war leader, a warrior with Power that made him a leader in battle. The warriors who rode with Geronimo believed that he could not be killed by bullets—which proved true enough although he was wounded many times. They also believed that he could foretell the future, and that he knew of events taking place far away—abilities he demonstrated to them repeatedly.

One American journalist penned a vivid description of Geronimo: "Crueler features were never cut. The nose is broad and heavy, the forehead low and wrinkled, the chin full and strong, the eyes like two bits of obsidian with a light behind them. The mouth is the most

This photo of Geronimo was taken at Canyon de los Embudos as General Crook tried to convince the last band of Chiricahua warriors to surrender. Photographer C. S. Fly took the only known photos of Apache warriors under arms in the field. *(Courtesy Arizona Historical Society, Tucson, Photo AHS 78,167)*

noticeable feature—a sharp, straight, thin-lipped gash of gener-
ous length and without one softening curve."

Geronimo seemed driven all of his life by the Apache code of
revenge, first against the Mexicans, then against the Americans.
His wife, mother, and children were killed in an attack on an
unsuspecting Apache camp by Mexican soldiers in the summer of
1858. In his autobiography dictated years later, he recalled:

> I found my aged mother, my young wife, and my three
> small children were among the slain. There were no
> lights in camp, so without being noticed, I silently
> turned away and stood by the river. How long I stood
> there I do not know . . . I stood until all had passed,
> hardly knowing what I would do. I had no weapons,
> nor did I hardly wish to fight, neither did I contemplate
> recovering the bodies of my loved ones . . . I did not
> pray, nor did I resolve to do anything in particular, for I
> had no purpose left. I finally followed the tribe silently,
> keeping just within hearing distance of the soft noise of
> the feet of the retreating Apaches . . . [Later, I] talked
> with the other Indians who had lost in the massacre, but
> none had lost as I had, for I had lost all. Within a few
> days, we arrived at our settlement. There were decora-
> tions that my wife Alope had made—and there were the
> playthings of our little ones. I burned them all . . . I was
> never again contented in our quiet home and whenever I
> saw anything to remind me of former happy days my
> heart would ache for revenge upon Mexico.

Geronimo probably instigated the breakout from the San Carlos
Reservation after Cibicu. Certainly, the massing of troops and the
executions of the scouts made all the Apache skittish. But Apache
indicate that one night while drunk, Geronimo mocked and criticized his nephew. The boy was so shamed that he killed himself.
Remorseful, and convinced that remaining on the reservation
would destroy his people, Geronimo fled its confines in September of 1881 with 74 Chiricahua and Nednhi, under the authority
of Juh and Natche. Chato, another aspiring war leader, also went
with them. Lozen, Nana, and Kaytennae either broke out with
Geronimo's group or had left the San Carlos Reservation earlier.

In any case, these three warriors with a handful of surviving Chihenne warriors joined the Chiricahua and the Nednhi in Juh's old haunts in the Sierra Madre. There, the small group of warriors resumed raiding.

Geronimo soon conceived a seemingly impossible plan—a raid back to San Carlos so that the small group of warriors could either free or abduct several hundred Apache from the reservation. The Apache left behind led by the noted chief Loco had refused to flee with Geronimo and the rest, but now the Chiricahua and Nednhi determined to get reinforcements so that they could reestablish the old, free life in the safety of the Sierra Madre.

APRIL 1882: RAID ON THE RESERVATION

The war party, led by Juh and Geronimo, struck the San Carlos Reservation in April of 1882. Jason Betzinez, a relative of Geronimo's and a member of Loco's band, left a compelling account in *I Fought with Geronimo*. "We saw a line of Apache warriors spread out along the west side of camp and coming our way with guns in their hands," recalled Betzinez. "Others were swimming horses across the river or pushing floating logs ahead of themselves. One of their leaders was shouting, 'take them all! No one is to be left in the camp. Shoot down anyone who refuses to go with us!' The suddenness of this attack, its surprise effect, and the inhuman order from one of the chiefs calling for the shooting of people of his own blood threw us into a tremendous flurry of excitement and fear." Chief of scouts Albert Sterling and about 15 of his men rode up as the Chiricahua begin herding Loco's band away from the reservation, but Geronimo and the rear guard killed Sterling and several of his men. "One of the warriors brought back Sterling's boots," recalled Betzinez. "This made me feel badly because Sterling had been a good friend of ours. He had often visited our camp and once taught me how to make a little wooden wagon."

Hundreds of women and children fled the reservation, guarded by the warriors. The fleeing Apache fought several running battles as they turned south and hurried toward their sanctuary in the Sierra Madre. In one of those fights, an old woman climbed up on top of a rock and called to her son—who she thought was among the Apache scouts guiding the soldiers. "In vain she called to him," recalled Betzinez. "Telling him that we had been run off against our will by the hostiles from Mexico. But her son wasn't there; and she was shot and killed." They all breathed a sigh of relief upon crossing into Mexico, although most of the warriors remained with the rear guard when they realized that the American soldiers had continued the pursuit into Mexico.

APRIL 30, 1882: DISASTER IN MEXICO

The women near the lead of the weary procession caught the smell of coffee and assumed that they were approaching an Apache encampment. Instead, the straggling line of mostly women and children ran into the Mexican Sixth Infantry Regiment under the command of Colonel Lorenzo Garcia. "We were suddenly attacked by the Mexican soldiers who came at us out of the ravine where they had been concealed," recalled Betzinez. "Almost immediately Mexicans were right among us all, shooting down women and children right and left. Here and there a few Indian warriors were trying to protect us while the rest of the band were running in all directions. It was a dreadful, pitiful sight, one that I shall never forget. People were falling and bleeding, and dying on all sides of us. Whole families were slaughtered on the spot, wholly unable to defend themselves. These were people who had never before been off the reservation, had never given any trouble."

The unarmed women and children ran for cover, while Geronimo marshaled a group of perhaps 32 warriors to halt the Mexican advance. "Bugle calls warned them when to expect a charge," Chihenne Apache James Kaywaykla told historian Eve

Ball. "Men sprang to the steps, fired, and sank back to reload. Women, too, used rifles. Cavalry came so close that one rider tumbled into the arroyo. Lozen, her head concealed by a screen of cactus, dropped a man with every shot. Three times the Mexicans charged, before deciding that the Apaches were not to be dislodged by that means. Toward evening, the Mexicans withdrew out of range, but their voices carried. They heard an officer say, 'Geronimo is in that ditch. Go in and get him.'"

Nearly out of ammunition, the Apache desperately needed a bag loaded with some 500 cartridges laying in the open in front of the ravine. An old woman volunteered to retrieve the ammunition, and ran into the open through a hail of Mexican bullets. "Bullets whistled about her but she never faltered. As she neared the arroyo she stumbled and fell, but did not loose her hold. She extended her feet toward the ditch and the men pulled both her and the precious bag into it. Lozen got up calmly and begin firing," recalled Kaywaykla. In the desperate fighting that ensued, a Chiricahua warrior named Fun distinguished himself. Twice, Fun jumped out of the ravine alone to meet a cavalry charge—seeming to dodge among the bullets, and breaking the charge, apparently because the Mexicans expected other warriors to follow him.

Finally, the Mexicans set fire to the grass, hoping to smoke out the Apache. Geronimo then acted in uncharacteristic fashion, according to Kaywaykla's account. Geronimo called out, "If we leave the women and children, we can escape." "What did you say?" demanded Fun, who Kaywaykla identifies as Geronimo's brother. "Repeat that," he said incredulously. "Come on!" cried Geronimo. "Let's go." Fun raised his rifle. "Say that again, and I'll shoot," he said. Geronimo then climbed to the rim of the arroyo and disappeared, leaving Fun and a handful of warriors to beat off the final charge of the Mexicans, according to Kaywaykla.

The Apache lost 78 that day, only 11 of them warriors. That night, Kaywaykla heard Loco and Nana talking, grieving over the losses. Nonetheless, Loco said the losses to disease and hunger from a summer at San Carlos would have been greater. The raid allowed the Apache to assemble the largest, free-living force since the days of Cochise and Mangas Coloradas—safe in the Sierra Madre. They quickly established virtual control of a large portion of northern Mexico, depopulating the area, stealing livestock at will, and forcing the residents to cluster around fortified settlements. The Mexican soldiers struck back, but they could rarely penetrate the forbidding Sierra Madre. The Apache set up boulder traps along the precarious trails into the mountains, so that they could wipe out a detachment of cavalry simply by rolling rocks down on them.

However, the deep divisions among the various Apache factions soon began to break up the large force. The ever-willful and independent Juh took his Nednhi to live separately. But his camp was hit several times by the Mexicans, sharply reducing his numbers. His warriors began to trickle away, perhaps concerned that the succession of defeats indicated that Juh had lost his war power. The divisions cut deeply between the Chihenne and the Chiricahua—especially between Loco's band and the warriors who had forced them to leave the reservation. Thus, the Apache force began breaking up almost as soon as the daring raid on San Carlos had assembled it.

SEPTEMBER 1882: GENERAL CROOK RETURNS

Meanwhile back in the United States, the escape of hundreds of Apache caused near hysteria. It also prompted the army to recall General Crook to resume command against the Apache. Crook immediately conducted an exhausting tour of the reservations, interviewing officers and soldiers and listening for hours to the complaints of the chiefs. He found himself mostly in agreement with the Indians, and appalled at the corruption of the reservation system. A grand jury issued a scathing indictment of San Carlos Agent Joseph Tiffany concluding that his administration was "a disgrace to the civilization of the age . . . As honest American citizens (we) express our abhorrence of the conduct of Agent

Tiffany and that class of reverend peculators who have cursed Arizona as Indian officials, and who have caused more misery and loss of life than all other causes combined . . . With the immense power wielded by the Indian agent almost any crime is possible. There seems to be no check upon his conduct." Despite the indictment, Tiffany was never convicted.

However, Crook found widespread abuses. He documented instances in which Indians who questioned the wagonloads of supplies that left the reservation were imprisoned without charges for more than a year at a time. He found that most of the supplies the government provided for the Indians were sold off the reservation, so that 20 Apache had to live for a week on a shoulder of beef and 20 cups of flour. Nonetheless, Tiffany persistently refused to allow the starving warriors to hunt off the reservation.

"Everywhere, the sullen, stolid, hopeless, suspicious faces of the older Indians challenge you," wrote Lieutenant Britton Davis, in *The Truth About Geronimo*. "You felt the challenge in your marrow—that unspoken challenge to prove yourself anything else than one more liar and thief, differing but little from the procession of liars and thieves who have preceded you."

Crook took immediate action. He reinstituted military control of the reservations. He fired many of the previous contractors. He put honest, sympathetic officers like Lieutenant Britton Davis and Captain Emmett Crawford in charge of the reservations. Davis soon discovered that the scales used to weigh beef cheated the government, and the Apache, of 1,500 pounds of beef each week. Crook also expelled all unauthorized people from the reservation. He issued metal identification tags to each Indian but also allowed them to settle anywhere on the reservation, instead of forcing them to cluster in mutually hostile groups near military posts.

"I believe that it is of far greater importance to prevent outbreaks than to attempt the difficult and sometimes hopeless task of quelling them after they do occur," Crook wrote. "Bad as the Indians often are, I have never yet seen one so demoralized that he was not an example in honor and nobility to the wretches who

Chato was a Chiricahua war leader who eventually became an army scout and Geronimo's bitter enemy. He served the army loyally but ended up in prison with Geronimo when the army banished all of the Chiricahua from the Southwest. *(Courtesy Arizona Historical Society, Tucson, Photo AHS 30,396)*

THE FATEFUL DEFECTION OF TSO-AY

As Chato's raiders completed their sweep and turned to head back toward the Sierra Madre, Tso-ay decided to return to the reservation. The Cibicu Apache warrior who had married into the Chiricahua band had lost his best friend in the raid. They had come upon an isolated camp and approached a silent tent. They'd called in English for anyone inside to come out, then filled the tent with bullet holes. Tso-ay and his friend raced toward the tent, only to meet a burst of gunfire. Tso-ay pivoted and ran for cover, but his friend dropped to the ground, already dead. The Apache rode on. They knew they could kill whoever waited in the tent, but they couldn't afford another loss or any more time. The whites could replace 100 soldiers easier than they could replace one warrior.

Now, standing on the ridgetop, tears glittering in his eyes, Tso-ay decided he'd had enough. "Friends," he'd told the listening warriors, "you know I have been with you all through this hard and dangerous raid. I have suffered when you suffered. I have been hungry when you were without food. Now I have lost my best friend. I cannot go on. I'm going to leave you and return to my old home country," according to an account of that pivotal moment left by Betzinez in *I Fought With Geronimo*. None of the listening warriors argued. Instead, they adhered to the Apache values of independence and individuality. "They gave him some things which would be useful to him when traveling alone. Then they said good-bye," reported Betzinez.

Tso-ay returned to the San Carlos Reservation, where Lieutenant Britton Davis and his Apache scouts quickly arrested him. Smiling shyly, the hauntingly handsome, light-skinned warrior dubbed "Peaches" for his complexion, reported that many of the Apache were willing to surrender. Tso-ay had survived years of warfare, which ultimately claimed both of his Chiricahua wives. But he'd always felt like an outsider among the Chiricahua whom General George Crook described as the "tigers of the human species." So he finally surrendered, although it meant leading the troops on a campaign to capture or kill the last of the free Apache.

Tzoe (or Tso-ay) defected from Chato's raiders and led General Crook into the Sierra Madre. A Cibicu Apache who married into the Chiricahua band, he felt mistreated by the Chiricahua and so helped the army. *(Courtesy Arizona Historical Society, Tucson, Photo AHS 4541)*

enrich themselves by plundering him of the little our government appropriates him."

Having pacified the Apache still on the reservations, Crook also began military preparations, knowing that the Chiricahua would eventually raid back into the United States. He improved the pack trains and dispatched independent, roving patrols to the border, looking for raiders. He posted guards on most of the water holes, knowing that the Chiricahua would eventually mount renewed raids into the United States. He also doubled the number of Apache scouts to a total of 250, understanding that the key to defeating Geronimo lay in turning his own people against him.

The expected raid soon came. A band of 26 warriors led by Chato and Bonito swept through Arizona and New Mexico in March of 1883, covering 400 miles in six days. The raiders killed 26 people, while losing only one warrior. They also killed a prominent local judge and his wife, kidnapping their little boy—Charlie McCombs. The killing and kidnapping sparked outrage throughout the territory. But the war party also suffered a fateful defection. Tso-ay—known to history as Peaches—left the war party and returned to the San Carlos Reservation to rejoin his relatives there. Crook soon learned of his return to the reservation, arrested him, and convinced him to guide an expedition into the Sierra Madre.

General Crook quickly assembled his force. He took six officers and 42 men of Company I, Sixth Cavalry. But his main fighting force consisted of 193 Apache scouts from many different bands including the Chiricahua under the command of Captain Crawford and Al Sieber. The company of scouts also included a translator—Mickey Free. Years ago, the kidnapping of this same half-Mexican, half-Apache boy had led to Cochise's decade-long war with the Americans.

Guided by Tso-ay, Crook's force made its way through the devastated northern provinces of Mexico and into the heart of the Sierra Madre. They passed abundant evidence of the toll imposed by the Chiricahua on every hand—discarded supplies, the bodies of cattle walked to death, butchered and abandoned, and even the sun-bleached skeletons of Mexican soldiers left where they'd fallen in their pursuit of the Apache into their most secure fortress. Bourke came to admire the fighting style and independence of the Apache warriors who trotted tirelessly up the rugged mountain range, easily outwalking the laboring horses of the cavalrymen.

> To the veterans of the campaigns of the Civil War, the loose straggling methods of the Apache scouts would appear startling, and yet no soldier would fail to apprehend at a glance that the Apache was the perfect, the ideal scout of the whole world. When Lieutenant Gatewood, the officer in command, gave the short, jerky order, Ugashe—Go—the Apaches started as if shot from a gun, and in a minute or less had covered a space of one hundred yards in front, which distance rapidly widened as they advanced at a rough, shambling walk. . . . They moved with no semblance of regularity; individual fancy alone governed . . . Their chests were broad, deep, and full; shoulders perfectly straight; limbs well-proportioned, strong and muscular without a suggestion of undue heaviness; hands and feet small and tapered but wiry; heads well-shaped, and countenances often lit up with a pleasant, good-natured expression, which would be more constant, perhaps, were it not for the savage, untamed cast imparted by the loose, disheveled gypsy locks of raven black, held away from the face by a broad, flat band of scarlet cloth. Their eyes were bright, clear, and bold, frequently expressive of the greatest good humor and satisfaction.

Crook soon realized that the slow-moving pack train could never move quickly enough through the maze of precipitous trails to surprise the Chiricahuas, so he sent about 150 Apache scouts on ahead under the command of Crawford and Sieber. Tso-ay guided them unerringly to Chato's camp. The scouts attacked immediately on May 15, killing nine and capturing five—although most of Chato's warriors were away hunting. The scouts found no sign of Charlie McCombs—the boy whose kidnapping had spurred such outrage in Arizona. Years later, Betzinez revealed the boy's fate. The first volley of the scouts had killed an old woman, whose enraged son seized the white child and dashed his brains out with a rock. The Apache then hid the body, for fear of retaliation.

Crook and his soldiers hurried forward and occupied Chato's camp. But Crook now found himself in a delicate situation, deep in the Sierra Madre, beyond any hope of relief. In fact, he was betting heavily on the demoralizing effect of his appearance here—guided by kinsmen of the Chiricahua.

As it happens, Geronimo was on his way back with a dozen Mexican women he had seized as hostages to trade for Apache captives. Betzinez relates an unsettling display of Geronimo's power: "Geronimo was sitting next to me with a knife in one hand and a chunk of beef . . . in the other. All at once he dropped the knife, saying 'Men, our people whom we left at our base camp are now in the hands of the U.S. troops! What shall we do?'" Furthermore, Geronimo accurately predicted when and where they would be met by a single warrior bearing news of the disastrous arrival of Crook's scouts.

But before Geronimo could return, women, children, and then warriors, including Loco and a Chiricahua chief named Chihuahua, began trickling into Crook's camp to surrender. Crook received each of the surrendering warriors with grave courtesy, freely sharing his supplies. However, the arrival of Geronimo, Kaytennae, and other hard-liners brought a deadly tension to the proceedings. "A fearful hubbub was heard in the tall cliffs overlooking camp," recalled Bourke in *An Apache Campaign in the Sierra Madres*. "Indians fully armed could be descried running about from crag to crag, evidently much perplexed and uncertain what to do."

Upon learning that Geronimo had arrived, General Crook hit upon a daring stratagem—designed to intimidate the hard-liners among the Chiricahua with a show of nonchalant personal courage. Taking his shotgun, he wandered away from camp alone—ostensibly to hunt birds. Warriors led by Geronimo and Kaytennae quickly surrounded him. Seemingly unconcerned, Crook sat down and opened negotiations. "(Geronimo) and his warriors were certainly as fine-looking a lot of pirates as ever cut a throat or scuttled a ship," observed Bourke. "Not one among them who was not able to travel forty to fifty miles a day over these gloomy precipices and along these gloomy canyons. In muscular development, lung and heart power, they were, without exception, the finest body of human beings I had ever looked upon . . . They are men of noticeable brain power, physically perfect and mentally acute—just the individuals to lead a forlorn hope in the face of every obstacle."

Crook bluffed boldly. He knew that the Chiricahua could simply melt away into the mountains and inflict heavy casualties on his retreating troops. But he affected an air of unconcern—explaining that he had merely come to give them a chance to surrender and return peacefully to the reservation. He would return soon with the Mexican Army, American soldiers, and with more Apache scouts to hunt down every remaining renegade.

Many of the Apache were relieved when this trusted enemy offered them a chance to surrender. "I am sure this was one of the happiest days of the year for General Crook," observed Betzinez. "We Apaches felt the same way about it. It was a great relief to give up to superior authority, to have some one take charge. No more worries, no more sleepless nights, fearing attacks by an enemy." Crook's arguments won over most of the Apache, forcing even Geronimo to yield. "I am not taking your arms from you," said Crook imperturbably, "because I am not afraid of you with them. You have been allowed to go about camp freely, merely to let you see that we have strength enough to exterminate you if we want to; and you have seen with your own eyes how many Apaches are fighting on our side and against you."

Geronimo insisted that he also wanted peace, and agreed to come to San Carlos in a month or two—after he had gathered up his scattered people. However, that night Geronimo convened a council of the leading warriors to convince them to stage a social dance for the Apache scouts. Upon a prearranged signal, the warriors would slaughter the unwary scouts. One leading warrior rose to oppose the idea—an enigmatic white warrior named Dji-li-kine who had been kidnapped as a baby and raised as an Apache. He scornfully dismissed Geronimo's plan—insisting that he had relatives

THE DEATH OF JUH

Juh remained in Mexico when most of the other Chiricahua and Chihenne holdouts returned to the reservation with General Crook. Juh had long ago had a vision that convinced him that he must never surrender, according to Juh's son, Ace Daklugie, who recounted the vision. Juh had assembled his warriors on a cliff overlooking a gorge in mountains they held sacred. As Juh lifted his arms and eyes in prayer, his people peered through the blue smoke of their campfire at the wall of the cliff across from their position.

"At first we saw nothing, but gradually a black spot appeared and seemed to grow larger and larger," recalled Daklugie, whose account was included in Eve Ball's *Indeh*. "It looked like an opening in the immense wall opposite us. It was the opening to a big cave, one inaccessible from the rim and equally so from below. Nothing but a bird could have reached the entrance to that cavern. As we watched, a thin white cloud descended and stopped just below the opening in the cliff. Every person knew this was a message from Ussen. "We have seen his sign," said Juh. "We watched as thousands of soldiers in blue uniforms began marching eight abreast into the great opening. This lasted for a long time, for there seemed to be an endless number of soldiers. The cave must have extended far into the cliff, for none returned."

The tribe called upon the medicine men to interpret the dream. "Ussen sent the vision to warn us that we will be defeated, and perhaps all killed by the government. Their strength in number, with their more powerful weapons, will make us indeed Indeh, the Dead. Eventually, they will exterminate us," said the medicine men. But Juh would not surrender—even to his God. "We must not give up. We must fight to the last man. We must remain free men or die fighting. There is no choice. I have nothing to offer you except death."

Juh died as he lived—unbroken and free. Riding along a riverbank with his sons, he suddenly fell from his horse into the water. Some accounts suggest he was drunk. But Daklugie said that he had not been drinking but suffered a stroke. His son held his head above the water, as his father died in his arms. His band buried him nearby, his grave unmarked.

among the scouts and would not attack them. He then stalked out of the council, crystallizing the opposition to the attack.

Supplies nearly exhausted, Crook set out on May 23, 1883, with 42 warriors and 273 women and children, mostly Apache who had been forced to leave the reservation. Loco, Nana, Kaytennae, Lozen, and Bonito went with Crook. Geronimo remained in Mexico, promising to come to the reservation within two months.

NOTES

pp. 100, 102 "Crueler features . . ." Roberts, p. 271.

p. 102 "I found my aged mother . . ." Miller, p. 281.

p. 103 "We saw a line of Apache warriors . . ." Jason Betzinez. *I Rode With Geronimo* (Lincoln: University of Nebraska Press, 1959), p. 56.

p. 104 "In vain she called . . ." Betzinez, p. 69.

pp. 104–5 "Bugle calls warned them . . ." Ball. *In the Days of Victorio*, p. 143.

p. 105 "If we leave the women . . ." Ball. *In the Days of Victorio*, p. 144.

pp. 106–7 "a disgrace to the civilization . . ." Bourke. *On the Border with Crook*, p. 443.

p. 107 "Everywhere, the sullen . . ." Davis, p. 114.

p. 107 "I believe that it is . . ." Bourke. *On the Border with Crook*, p. 438.

p. 112 "To the veterans . . ." John Bourke. *An Apache Campaign in the Sierra Madres* (1886; reprint, Lincoln: University of Nebraska Press), p. 21.

pp. 113–14 "Geronimo was sitting next . . ." Betzinez, p. 113.

p. 114 "(Geronimo) and his warriors . . .' Bourke. *Apache Campaign*, pp. 85–86.

p. 114 "I am sure . . ." Betzinez, p. 116.

p. 114 "I am not taking your arms . . ." Bourke. *Apache Campaign*, p. 95.

p. 115 "At first we saw . . ." Ball. *Indeh.* p. 76.

GERONIMO'S WAR

1884–1886

Crook returned to mixed reactions. Many people had given up his command for dead, reasoning that Crook's reliance on Apache scouts had finally proved fatal. When he emerged from Mexico with most of the renegades in tow, he was greeted as a hero in some quarters. Others bitterly criticized him for letting Geronimo remain behind. In reality, Crook's expedition to the Sierra Madre had finally broken the Apache resistance. They would never again live as a free people. But it had also opened the door to additional years of conflict and the most famous phase of the long Apache wars—thanks to Geronimo's stubborn persistence. Geronimo finally showed up in February of 1884, with 16 warriors and 70 women and children. Crook put the Chiricahua under the supervision of Lieutenant Britton Davis who quickly came to respect and sympathize with them, marveling at their philosophical acceptance of their fate.

> In my talks with the Indians, they showed no resentment of the way they had been treated in the past—only wonderment at the why of it. They had been shifted from reservation to reservation; told to farm and had their crops destroyed; assured that the government would ration them, then left to half starve; herded in the hot malarial river bottoms of the Gila and San Carlos when they were mountain people. These and other

questions I could not answer. Above all, they wondered if they would now be allowed to live in peace. Poor Devils. Their fears were realized. In two years, they were in prisons in Florida—four hundred innocent people, men, women, and children, who had kept faith with us, punished for the guilt of Chihuahua and two or three other malcontents.

Chiefly, Davis blamed Geronimo, whose persistent refusal to remain on the reservation brought the government's wrath down on the heads of all the Chiricahua. "He was neither a chief nor a subchief. He had risen to leadership of a faction of the warriors by sheer courage, determination and skill as a leader. But he was feared and disliked by a great majority of the Indians," wrote Davis, in *The Truth About Geronimo*. Still, Davis sympathized with the plight of the Apache. "In treachery, broken pledges on the part

Geronimo (left) and Naiche, posed on horseback during negotiations at Canyon de Los Embudos in March of 1886, another in the famous C. S. Fly series of photos. *(Courtesy Arizona Historical Society, Tucson, Photo AHS 78,162)*

This woman, thought to be a spy for the army on the reservation, had her nose cut off, the standard Apache punishment for adultery. Lieutenant Britton Davis's attempt to curtail wife beating and drinking led to a breakout from the reservation. *(Courtesy Arizona Historical Society, Tucson, Photo AHS 25,633)*

of high officials, lies, thievery, slaughter of defenseless women and children, and every crime in the catalogue of man's inhumanity to man the Indian was a mere amateur compared to the 'noble white man.' His crimes were retail, ours wholesale. We learned his methods in that line and with our superior intelligence, improved upon them."

THE RESPECT OF AN ENEMY

A few times in the grim record of the relentless war against the Apache, someone opened his eyes to the humanity of his enemy, but not often. One such transformation is documented in the memoir of Lieutenant Britton Davis, who General Crook placed in charge of the renegade Chiricahua when they returned to the reservation. Davis noted that the Chiricahua actually seemed more friendly to him than to the other Apache bands. Davis commented:

> The Chiricahua and Warm Springs who had come in were hated and feared by the other Indians of the Reservation . . . and seemed to turn to us for reassurance and comforting. Daily, half a dozen or more would be found hanging around our buildings, anxious for a talk and a smoke. Our relations with the other Indians had been rather formal. The hostiles were different, and we soon came to feel toward some of them as we would feel toward any other class of people. In fact, we begin to find them decidedly human. Much to my surprise, I found that they had a keen sense of humor and were not averse to telling jokes on themselves as well as others.

Most proved willing to adapt to life on the reservation—even hitching their stocky, near-wild war ponies to plows and wagons—with often hilarious results.

> I honestly believe some of [the ponies] could have crawled through the harnesses put on them if given a little time." By stuffing the collars with anything available in the way of old rags, cutting the harnesses to shreds, and with the assistance of half a dozen Indians to each pony, a wagon would finally be hitched up, the proud proprietor would mount it, seize the reins, and away he would go over the plain at full tilt, his erstwhile assistants scrambling into the tail end of the wagon as it passed them on the run. The Indians, whooping and laughing, were getting as much fun out of the circus as we were . . . The ponies preferred to trot or gallop, and the plowpoints were oftener above the ground than in it. Now and then a point would strike a hidden root or stump; then the plowman would execute a somersault over the plow handles, to the great delight of his friends. The plow trail, when completed, had the regularity of the trail of a snail on a bat.

> Gradually, Davis became one of the handful of whites who saw the Apache as people, rather than savages. "My feelings toward them began to change. That ill-defined impression that they were something a little better than animals but not quite human; something to be on your guard against; something to be eternally watched with suspicion and killed with no more compunction than one would kill a coyote; the feeling that there could be no possible ground upon which we could meet as man to man, passed away."

But despite Davis's best efforts, tensions built on the reservation. Davis became the focal point of struggling factions. On one side, Chato, Tso-ay, Mickey Free, and others worked closely with Davis—gaining power in the closed system of the reservation. Davis established a network of informers, who brought him worrisome rumors of disaffection. Gradually, Chato, Tso-ay, and Mickey Free convinced Davis that Geronimo and the hard-liners were plotting to murder him and bolt the reservation. Geronimo, Kaytennae, Nana, and Chihuahua remained apart, viewing Davis with deep suspicion. They believed Chato and the others frequently made up rumors and provided misleading translations to turn Davis against them.

Davis soon came to view Kaytennae as a dangerous man. "Kaytennae made no effort to get on friendly terms with us. We would find him standing silent and alone near an open window, or at a corner of the building, or near a doorway; watchful, but surly and unresponsive when spoken to. Either he was exceptionally curious or exceptionally suspicious. Probably both," wrote Davis. Davis's informants soon warned him of planned breakouts, and even an incident in which Kaytennae nearly assassinated Davis when the officer almost stumbled upon a group of warriors on a forbidden drinking binge. Kaywaykla brands that story as a lie, intended to spur Kaytennae's arrest.

If so, it worked. In the summer of 1884, Davis called for 140 troopers from nearby Fort Apache and hid them in the woods behind his council tent as backup for the arrest of Kaytennae. But the next day the chiefs showed up with many armed warriors, including Kaytennae's contingent of 30 men. Davis boldly confronted Kaytennae, branded him a troublemaker, and insisted that he go to Fort Apache for punishment. Kaytennae demanded the names of his accusers, but Davis refused. Kaytennae wheeled and returned to his men, who cocked their rifles and advanced. Davis scouts cocked their own guns.

"The situation was not one I can recommend for jumpy nerves," Davis recalled. "To me it seemed a three-cornered bet as to who would get me—Kaytennae's band, the Indians around me, or the troops in the rear." Kaytennae then returned with his men to again confront Davis. "Trembling with rage so that he could hardly speak, he demanded that I should point out to him which of his men had accused him," wrote Davis. "He had weakened, and there would be no fight." Davis stepped forward, and boldly unbuckled Kaytennae's gun belt, displaying that confidence and personal courage essential to dealing with warriors.

Kaytennae was tried on vague charges, although he wasn't in the courtroom, and sentenced to hard labor at Alcatraz in San Francisco Bay. General Crook hoped that the exposure to the full power of white civilization would turn Kaytennae into an advocate for peace. So Kaytennae was kept at hard labor in Alcatraz for the first year, then allowed virtually free run of San Francisco.

In the meantime, tensions on the reservation continued to build, especially when Davis tried to implement Crook's orders forbidding use of alcohol and wife beating. The Apache prized fidelity, although women were free to divorce their husbands. Tradition demanded that a man whose wife had shamed him by being unfaithful should cut off her nose. Apache accounts suggest that in free-living Apache bands children were virtually never hit and wife beating was very rare. However, domestic violence apparently became much more common on the reservation, due to the prevalence of alcohol abuse and the demeaning loss of status for warriors.

Matters came to a head on May 15, 1884, when the leaders gathered outside Davis's tent, determined to air their grievances before the young lieutenant. Loco begin to harangue him in his ponderous, long-winded way. Then Chihuahua jumped to his feet and interrupted, a startling breech of Apache etiquette. "What I have to say can be said in a few words," exclaimed the excited Chihuahua, "then Loco can talk all the rest of the day if he wants to." He then went on to vigorously protest Davis's interference with Apache domestic life.

Davis repeated the edict, reproaching the chiefs for the way they treated their women. Nana, face grim as a thunderhead, barked something at Davis. Mickey Free pointedly avoided translating, but Davis insisted. "Tell the Nantan Enchan (stout chief)," Mickey Free translated slowly, "that he can't advise me how to treat my woman. He is only a boy. I killed men before he was born." Chihuahua then said that every one of the chiefs had been drinking tizwin the night before. "We all drank tizwin last night. All of us in the tent and outside except the scouts. What are you going to do about it? Are you going to put us all in jail? You have no jail big enough, even if you could put us all in jail."

Davis told the angry chiefs that he would ask General Crook what he should do, knowing that the chiefs both respected and feared Crook. However, Davis's telegram was never relayed to General Crook. Instead, the fearful chiefs waited without word for several days, until they convinced themselves that Davis would soon have them arrested and executed.

On May 17, 1884, 35 warriors, eight boys old enough to fight, and 10 women and children fled the reservation—including Geronimo, Chihuahua, Natche, Mangas, Nana, and probably Lozen. Geronimo helped stampede the others by telling them that he had sent warriors to kill Davis and Chato. Convinced they would be executed for those killings, Chihuahua and Mangas joined the breakout. Later, they discovered that the warriors sent to kill Davis found him surrounded by the scouts and so fled without attacking. Furious that he had been tricked, Chihuahua broke away from Geronimo and the others.

Davis tracked Chihuahua and fought a sharp engagement. Committed now, Chihuahua turned his warriors and headed on down into Mexico—covering 90 miles without stopping. Meanwhile, Geronimo and Natche's band surprised a military supply train in Skeleton Canyon near the Mexican border, killing three soldiers and capturing horses, mules, and plenty of ammunition.

Crook marshaled thousands of troops and posted guards at every water hole between San Carlos and the border. A company of scouts led by Chato caught up to Geronimo's rear guard, fought

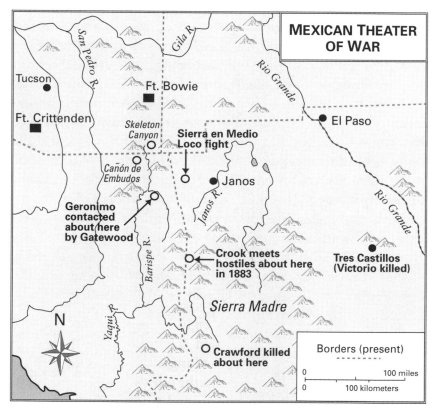

This map shows the location of the key events in the final stages of the Apache wars, including the site of Victorio's death, the site where Loco's fleeing band was ambushed by Mexican troops, the place Geronimo met with Lieutenant Gatewood, and Skeleton Canyon where Geronimo surrendered for the last time.

a brief battle, then lost them. Captain Crawford pursued them on into Mexico, and an advanced detachment of 30 scouts led by Chato caught up to them once again, capturing 15 women and children and 54 horses the hostiles had stolen from the army.

The soldiers maintained the pursuit for weeks, moving freely across the border. Davis's detachment crossed into Mexico and covered 500 miles through tough terrain, finally returning to American soil nearly horseless and dressed in rags without ever having gotten more than a glimpse of the fleeing Chiricahua. Disgusted and worn out, Davis resigned his commission. Crawford stayed on their trail for four months, covering more than 1,000 miles, during which time he killed three of the hostiles and captured 30—thanks entirely to the efforts of his Apache scouts.

Incredibly, in the midst of this pursuit— Chihuahua's younger brother, Ulzanna, slipped away with a dozen warriors, doubled back into the United States, and attacked the Camp Apache Reservation—killing several Apache, kidnapping several women, and stealing several horse herds. He then ambushed a cavalry patrol and returned to Mexico. The raiders covered 1,200 miles in four weeks, killed 38 people, and stole 250 horses with the loss of only one warrior.

Crawford's Apache scouts pushed on down into Mexico toward the Sierra Madre, still hoping to bring Geronimo to bay. Deep in Mexico in January 1886, Crawford encountered a troop of Mexican irregulars, commanded by a renowned scalp hunter. The Mexicans begin firing on Crawford's Apache scouts. Crawford climbed to the top of a boulder to stop the fight but was almost immediately shot in the head. The enraged scouts returned fire, killing the Mexican commander and a dozen others. Geronimo watched the fight from a mountainside, laughing and shaking his head. Lieutenant Mario Maus managed to finally stop the battle, but Crawford died five days later.

Geronimo then sent Lozen and another woman down to talk to Maus, cautiously opening negotiations. Geronimo agreed to meet with General Crook at the Canyon de los Embudos, just below the Mexican border. In March 1886, Crook and Geronimo began

THE SURRENDER OF THE CHIRICAHUA

General Crook and Geronimo became bitter, personal enemies in their long battle. Small wonder, Geronimo's refusal to surrender ultimately led to Crook's virtual firing, and Crook's use of the scouts doomed the Apache resistance. Their hatred, and Crook's ability to divide his enemies and isolate Geronimo, were all evident in Captain John Bourke's record of the negotiations at Canyon de los Embudos.

Geronimo found himself unsettled by Crook's stern manner, and complained that Mickey Free, Chato, and Lieutenant Davis had forced him to flee the reservation by spreading lies. "What is the matter that you don't speak to me and look with a pleasant face; it would make better feeling ... why don't you look at me and smile at me? I am the same man; I have the same feet, legs, and hands, and the sun looks down on me a complete man; I wish you would look and smile at me. The Sun, the Darkness, the Winds, are all listening to what we say now."

But Crook replied: "I have heard what you said. It seems very strange that more than forty men should be afraid of three; but if you left the reservation for that reason, why did you kill innocent people, sneaking all over the country to do it? What did those innocent people do to you that you should kill them, steal their horses, and slip around in the rocks like coyotes? What had that to do with killing innocent people? There is not a week passes that you don't hear foolish stories in your own camp; but you are no child—you don't have to believe them. You promised me in the Sierra Madre that peace would last, but you have lied about it. ... Everything you did on the reservation is known; there is no use for you to try to talk nonsense. I am no child. You must make up your minds whether you will stay out on the warpath or surrender unconditionally. If you stay out, I'll keep after you and kill the last one if it takes fifty years."

The negotiations continued for days, most of the Chiricahua warriors remaining in their virtually impregnable position. Eventually, Crook wore them down—playing skillfully on the divisions between Chihuahua and Geronimo. Chihuahua broke first, according to Bourke's rendering of the negotiations.

It is as you say: we are always in danger out here. I hope that from this one we may live better with our families, and not do any more harm to anybody. I am anxious to behave. I think that the Sun is looking down upon me, and the Earth is listening. I am thinking better. It seems to me that I have seen the one who makes the rain and sends the winds, or he must have sent you to this place. I surrender myself to you, because I believe in you and you do not deceive us . . . I want you to be a father to me, and treat me as your son. I want you to have pity on me. . . . I am now in your hands. I place myself at your disposition to dispose of as you please.

negotiations. Crook found the Chiricahua camped on a small hill surrounded by deep ravines, a place impossible to surround or surprise. They met in a cottonwood-shaded ravine between the two encampments, with Geronimo careful to send no more than half a dozen warriors at one time to meet with the Americans. Crook brought with him a small detachment of soldiers and scouts, including Kaytennae—recently returned from his stint in Alcatraz. Crook hoped that Kaytennae would help convince the warriors to surrender. Kaywaykla indicated that his father joined the scouts in order to counter Chato. "White Eyes may have had delusions as to the purpose of Kaytennae in joining the scouts, but the Apaches did not," noted Kaywaykla. "Kaytennae went along to see that the interpreters were honest and that Chato was held in check."

Geronimo blamed the troubles mostly on Chato, Mickey Free, Lieutenant Davis, and lies written about him in the newspapers, according to Bourke's account in *On the Border with Crook*. Geronimo said he had prayed to the Dawn (Tapida) and the Darkness, to the Sun (Chigo-na-ay) and the Sky (Yandestan), and to Assunutlije to help him put a stop to the bad stories told about him. But Crook's skillful blend of threats and promises soon convinced the Apache leaders to surrender. Geronimo could not hold out alone, especially after his chief—Natche—decided to give up.

"I give myself up to you," Geronimo told Crook after days of negotiation. "Do with me what you please. I surrender. Once I

Santiago McKinn (front and center) was an 11-year-old white boy kidnapped by the Apache six months before the negotiations at Canyon de los Embudos. He wept inconsolably at the prospect of being taken from the Apache and restored to his family.

moved about like the wind. Now I surrender to you. That is all." However, the Chiricahua's surrender was not unconditional. Actually, Crook promised they would be reunited with their families and imprisoned for two years away from the reservation. After that time, they could return to the reservation with all of their crimes forgiven.

But that night, a whisky peddler slipped into the Chiricahua camp. The warriors got roaring drunk, while listening to the peddler's warnings that Geronimo and the other leaders would be promptly hung if they returned to the United States. Drunk and frightened, Geronimo, Natche, 20 warriors, 13 women, and 6 children fled into the night. Crook returned with the rest of the Chiricahua, to a firestorm of criticism.

APRIL 2, 1886: CROOK RESIGNS

General Philip Sheriden, Crook's commander, disavowed the conditions Crook had offered his captives, and harshly criticized him for letting Geronimo escape. Sheriden implied treachery on the part of Crook's scouts and ordered him to stop using Apache scouts. Indignant, Crook offered his resignation on April 1, 1886. General Sheridan accepted it the next day. "I believe the plan upon which I have conducted operations is the one most likely to prove successful in the end. It may be however that I am too much wedded to my own views in this matter and as I have spent nearly eight years in the hardest work of my life in this department, I respectfully request that I now be relieved from its command," concluded Crook.

Sheridan appointed General Nelson Miles in Crook's place, putting at his disposal 5,000 soldiers, representing an astonishing one-quarter of the American army. Miles, a politically astute, vainglorious, ambitious man, realized that his career now rode on catching less than two dozen Apache warriors. He took immediate action. Miles mustered out almost all of the Apache scouts, sending them back to the reservations. He established a

General Crook meets with the Apache leaders at Canyon de los Embudos to negotiate their surrender. Geronimo (third from left) initially agreed to surrender but then slipped away—spurring Crook's resignation. *(Courtesy Arizona Historical Society,*

heliograph system, using polished mirrors on mountaintops to flash messages to coordinate troop movements. The system could send a message 2,500 miles and get a reply in the space of four hours. He organized his 5,000 soldiers to provide continuous coverage of a huge area—patrolling the border, crossing freely into Mexico, and staking out watering holes.

But Geronimo's warriors made a mockery of all of Miles's preparations, raiding with seeming impunity throughout Arizona and New Mexico. The soldiers rarely got close enough to shoot at the warriors. Seven times soldiers did manage to capture Geronimo's horses and supplies. But that proved but a minor inconvenience to the Apache, who could outwalk the soldiers' horses. The warriors simply melted into the landscape, stole new horses, and regrouped at the rendezvous points they established before each day's camp. One hand-picked cavalry troop of 100 men and 20 scouts under the command of Captain Henry Lawton covered 1,400 miles in four months without ever forcing Geronimo to turn and fight.

Geronimo, in his autobiography, recalled that long, grim flight to nowhere. "We were reckless with our lives, because we felt that every man's hand was against us. If we returned to the reservation we would be put in prison and killed; if we stayed in Mexico they would continue to send soldiers to fight us; so we gave no quarter to anyone and asked no favors."

Desperate, Miles eventually turned secretly to Lieutenant Charles Gatewood—one of the few officers still in the service who had commanded a company of Apache scouts. General Miles ordered Gatewood to take two Apache scouts with relatives among Geronimo's band into Mexico to try to convince Geronimo to surrender. Gatewood enlisted George Wratton as his interpreter, knowing that the Apache considered him a friend.

Gatewood and his small party traveled deep into Mexico, until they picked up Geronimo's trail. Kieta and Martine, the two Apache scouts, then climbed a rugged mountain where Geronimo's band had taken refuge. Seeing them coming, Geronimo prepared to shoot them—not wanting to hear new surrender terms. But Fun intervened, with the support of the relatives of the scouts in Geronimo's band. Reluctantly, Geronimo agreed to meet with Gatewood.

The warriors came to the meeting place—Geronimo among the last. He shook Gatewood's hand, and asked about his sickly appearance. Gatewood passed around a bag of tobacco, and offered Miles's terms: They could surrender and be sent to prison with the other Chiricahua in Florida for two years. They would then be allowed to return to the San Carlos Reservation. "Accept these terms, or fight it out to the bitter end," said Gatewood.

A long silence fell over the warriors. Geronimo insisted they be allowed to return to the reservation in Arizona without undergoing a period of exile. Gatewood reiterated the terms. He then revealed that Chihuahua's band had already been sent to Florida, which seemed to break down the warriors' resistance—knowing they would never see their relatives again unless they yielded. At last, Geronimo asked what sort of man General Miles was—wondering whether he could trust him. "We want your advice," said Geronimo. "Consider yourself not a white man, but one of us. Remember all that has been said today and tell us what we should do."

"Trust the general," said Gatewood, although he probably knew that Miles would not keep his word. "Surrender to him." Reluctantly, Geronimo agreed, but only if General Miles would meet with him personally in Skeleton Canyon. Miles finally showed up on September 3, 1886. Geronimo rode down from his well-defended campsite, dismounted, and shook Miles's hand.

The interpreter said: "General Miles is your friend." Geronimo replied: "I never saw him, but I have been in need of friends. Why has he not been with me?" Everyone within earshot broke into laughter—although given Geronimo's legendary lack of humor, he might have been perfectly serious. Miles later recorded his impression of Geronimo: "He was one of the brightest, most resolute, determined looking men that I have ever encountered. He had the clearest, sharpest, dark eye I think I have ever seen."

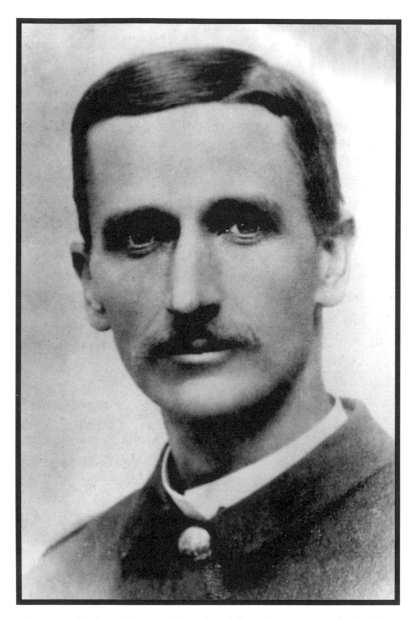

Lieutenant Charles B. Gatewood convinced Geronimo to surrender for the final time. Gatewood performed heroic service leading troops of Apache scouts, but he was shunted to the side in the unseemly scramble by his superiors to take credit for Geronimo's capture. Broken in health, injured in a dynamite explosion, he died in relative obscurity. *(Courtesy Arizona Historical Society, Tucson, Photo AHS 1160)*

The next morning, Miles made a ceremony of Geronimo's surrender—after reiterating the terms that Gatewood had offered. Miles picked up two stones, drew a line in the dirt, and said condescendingly to the war leader: "This represents the ocean," he said, indicating the line. He placed a stone next to it. "This represents the place where Chihuahua is with his band." Then he placed at a distance a second stone representing Geronimo and a third representing the Chiricahua still on the reservation. Finally, he picked up all three stones and placed them together. "That is what the President wants to do, get all of you together."

Geronimo recalled the surrender: "We stood between his troopers and my warriors. We placed a large stone on the blanket before us. Our treaty was made by this stone and it was to last until the stone should crumble to dust; so we made the treaty, and bound each other with an oath."

The entourage set out for Fort Bowie, 60 miles away. Geronimo gazed at the Chiricahua Mountains, where he had defied his enemies for a lifetime. "This is the fourth time I have surrendered," he said sorrowfully. "And I think it is the last time," Miles interjected immediately.

A few days later, on September 8, 1886, soldiers loaded Geronimo's band onto railway cars for the journey to Florida. Already, the rest of the Chiricahua had been rounded up and herded onto cattle cars. Some 381 Chihenne and Chiricahua Apaches were imprisoned. That included 17 Apache scouts who had served the army loyally, even helping to hunt down Geronimo. Eskiminzin was included in the roundup, and the prosperous farm he had built up confiscated and distributed without payment to white settlers. Chato was in Washington, D.C., with a delegation of Chiricahua scouts, pleading for their people when Geronimo surrendered. He was still proudly wearing the impressive medal he'd received when the train carrying the scouts home was diverted to prison at Leavenworth, Kansas. Chato and the others were eventually imprisoned with Geronimo first in Florida, then in Alabama, and finally at Fort Sill, Oklahoma.

General Nelson A. Miles deployed thousands of soldiers to catch Geronimo, but he finally had to rely on Apache scouts to convince Geronimo to surrender by offering terms Miles knew he couldn't keep.   *(Courtesy Arizona Historical Society, Tucson, Photo AHS 1923)*

A small crowd gathered to witness the end of an epoch in the West. The Apache prisoners stared impassively at the crowd—Geronimo whose resistance had proved so costly to both his enemies and his friends, Lozen whose powers had helped her people fight, Natche who had tried so hard to hold on to the land of his father, Tzo-ay who had yearned for home and trusted the wrong side, and even Martine and Kieta who received an indefinite prison term instead of the promised reward for convincing Geronimo to surrender. As the train pulled away, a military band struck up a dirgelike tune—a mocking rendition of "Auld Lang Syne."

1886–1913: THE LAST BETRAYAL

Months of confusion ensued, since Miles refused to reveal to his superiors the terms of the surrender he had offered Geronimo. President Grover Cleveland initially insisted Geronimo be turned over to civilian authorities for trial—but Miles blocked that decision by sending them all to Florida. Miles proved so evasive, that the government was finally forced to stop the train and question the Chiricahua themselves to find out on what terms they had surrendered. Geronimo said that Miles had promised that the Chiricahua would be reunited with their families on a beautiful reservation in the East and held there for two years before being allowed to return to Arizona.

But the government refused to honor those surrender terms. Geronimo's warriors were imprisoned at Fort Pickens, Florida, while their relatives taken from the San Carlos Reservation were imprisoned at Fort Marion, Florida. Geronimo's warriors were not reunited with their families for more than a year, when the Chiricahua were all moved to Mount Vernon Barracks, Alabama, in May of 1888. They remained there for six years, while disease and despair took their toll. The 119 deaths represented one-quarter of Apache who had been loaded into the cattle cars in 1886. The surviving Chiricahua were allowed to move to the Kiowa reservation at Fort Sill in Oklahoma's Indian Territory in 1894.

Meanwhile, the scouts and their families lived among the families of the people they'd hunted. Chato, hated by Geronimo and his followers, lived apart from most of the rest of the band. Tso-ay befriended Captain Bourke, who became a noted anthropologist, and provided invaluable information on Apache beliefs and culture. In the 1930s, he served as an informant for another famous archeologist. Those divisions persist to this day, with the descendants of scouts forever estranged from the descendants of the last renegades. Ace Daklugie captured the bitterness, loss, and futility of this tragic war of the Apaches. An apprentice warrior when he was captured, Daklugie sat hopelessly on the railway car bearing him to exile. When the train halted, he braced himself for summary execution. Instead, he watched as the white soldiers loaded onto the train the scouts who had helped hunt down the last renegades. "That was the one good thing about the whole process," he said. "The scouts who had betrayed their people were doomed to captivity like the rest of us," he told historian Eve Ball in *Indeh*.

General Crook, Captain Bourke, and other supporters lobbied to improve the condition of their imprisonment and to secure their return to the Southwest. Crook was especially incensed at the imprisonment of the scouts and the Chiricahua who had remained on the San Carlos Reservation. He noted the scouts "were of more value in hunting down and compelling the surrender of the renegades than all other troops engaged in operations against them combined . . . During the entire course of operations against them . . . the only hostiles killed or captured were in encounters with the scouts alone, except for two men." Every successful encounter was "due exclusively to the exertions of the scouts . . . It was the unanimous testimony of officers commanding scout companies that the Chiricahuas were the most subordinate, energetic, untiring, and by odds, the most efficient in their command."

In captivity, Geronimo's fame mushroomed. He took up farming, joined the Dutch Reformed Church, dictated his autobiography, and worked as a healer among his people. He also appeared in national expositions, made money selling signed photographs and tourist knickknacks, and rode in Theodore Roosevelt's inaugural parade. But as long as he lived, the government refused any proposal that would return the Chiricahua to New Mexico or Arizona.

After Geronimo's death of pneumonia in 1909, the government decided to use a portion of the Fort Sill Reservation for an artillery range and agreed to move the Chiricahua back to the Southwest. The Chiricahua and Chihenne survivors sent a delegation to Warm Springs to scout it as a possible reservation site but decided it was now too barren because of the effects of decades of grazing and mining. So they elected instead to join their old allies the Mescalero in New Mexico, who welcomed them back to the Southwest. About one-third of the Chiricahua decided to stay with their farms in Oklahoma while two-thirds sold most of their goods and boarded the train for New Mexico after 27 years captivity as prisoners of war.

NOTES

pp. 117–18 "In my talks . . ." Davis, p. 114.

pp. 118–19 "He was neither a chief . . ." Davis, p. 113.

p. 120 "The Chiricahua and Warm Springs . . ." Davis, p. 72.

p. 120 "I honestly believe . . ." Davis, p. 103.

p. 121 "My feelings toward them . . ." Davis, p. 111.

p. 121 "Kaytennae made no effort . . ." Davis, p. 123.

p. 123 "What I have to say . . ." Davis, p. 144. (Davis recorded the dialogue in this section sometime after the events described.)

p. 126 "What is the matter . . ." Roberts, p. 269.

p. 127 "It is as you say . . ." Roberts, p. 271.

p. 127 "White eyes may . . ." Ball. *Days of Victorio*, p. 200.

pp. 127–28 "I give myself up to you . . ." Roberts, p. 272.

p. 129 "I believe the plan . . ." Roberts, p. 275.

p. 130 "We were reckless . . ." Miller, p. 283.

p. 131   "Accept these terms . . ." Worcester, p. 302.

p. 131   "General Miles is your friend . . ." Roberts, p. 295.

p. 131   "He was one of the . . ." Roberts, p. 296.

p. 133   "This represents the ocean . . ." Roberts, p. 296.

p. 133   "We stood between his troopers . . ." Roberts, p. 296.

p. 133   "This is the fourth time . . ." Roberts, p. 296.

p. 136   "were of more value . . ." Worcester, p. 314.

EPILOGUE

▲

SOLVING THE PUZZLE

Looking back, conflict between the Americans in the grip of their imagined destiny and the Apache defending their homeland seems as though it were inevitable. Wandering Apache bands each claimed a vast area, lived in part on plunder taken from others, and defended their territory. The aggressive, expansionist Americans came armed with an ideology and economic system that impelled them to take possession of the continent.

But why the wars lasted so long and flared again each time they seemed settled poses more of a puzzle. Even today, more than a century after Geronimo's warriors were loaded onto cattle cars, most of the land they fought for with such devotion and passion remains empty. Miners have mostly come and gone. The farmers and city builders mostly confine themselves to a few low, flat areas of Arizona and New Mexico—leaving the mountains the Apache claimed mostly untenanted. The Dragoon and Chiricahua Mountains that Howard promised to Cochise are used only by hikers, campers, and scattered cattle ranchers who only remain in business because of government grazing subsidies. The area around Ojo Caliente, where Victorio yearned to live out his life, is also mostly empty.

In truth, the failure of the peacemakers and the persistence of the violence grew from many roots including bureaucracy, economics, racism, and the self-perpetuating nature of violence itself. The Apache belief in the importance of revenge and the American refusal to extend equal rights and justice to the Apache combined to sow the wind with violence, reaping the whirlwind of death.

Partly, the failure of the peacemakers stemmed from bureaucracy. Repeatedly, fair-minded, far-sighted American leaders demonstrated that they understood the problem. The whole war could have been averted if the Americans had simply established reasonable reservations based on the home territories of individual bands and then provided just compensation for the land taken from the Apache. Some raiding probably would have continued for a generation or two as the Apache adjusted to the cultural impact of the curtailment of raiding and warfare. But the Americans could have responded to such raids by punishing individuals instead of entire bands—and by turning to the Apache leaders to help police the peace. Instead, the vagaries of American politics and bureaucracy repeatedly frustrated far-sighted policy making. Congress persistently failed to support the efforts of the peacemakers in the field, either not ratifying treaties or not providing the rations that would make it possible for the Apache to abandon raiding without starving. Moreover, Congress also repeatedly shifted control of the reservations from the army to the Indian Bureau and back again, spawning corruption and abuses that undercut all efforts to keep the Apache peacefully settled on reservations. Worst of all, the government virtually guaranteed decades of bitter warfare by abandoning its promises and concentrating mutually hostile Apache bands on a few inadequate reservations.

Partly, the failure to achieve peace arose from the actions of individuals. On the Apache side, war leaders like Geronimo, Victorio, and Delshay showed that they preferred death to unconditional surrender and loss of their homelands. Even when they understood the hopelessness of their cause, they led the resistance—inspiring many others to join them. On the American side, gifted and sympathetic officers like General Crook, Captain John Bourke, and Colonel Kit Carson followed orders and found ways to break the Apache resistance—even when they sympathized with their enemies and criticized their own government. In addition, corrupt contractors, scalp hunters, whisky peddlers, and others continued to provoke Apache resistance for personal profit, although they fully understood the consequences.

Economics also frustrated the efforts to make peace. The Apache were trapped by their reliance on raiding and hunting. That left them with few options when the Americans drastically reduced the available game and forbade raiding. Even when the Apache wanted to surrender—they found that the abandonment of raiding sentenced them to starvation on the reservations. Greed and capitalism drove the conflict on the American side. Sometimes, the lust for riches seemed almost demented, as prospectors wandered alone through Apache territory despite the threat of death and torture. Army leaders often advocated letting the Apache alone on large reservations, but the constant influx of settlers and prospectors seeking riches doomed that effort.

Finally, the conflict remained cultural and racial. Both sides considered their opponents barely people, not entitled to the rights and respect due to a real person. Apache killed many whites who had done nothing to them, often resorting to torture and mutilation of the bodies. They did adopt captive women and children into their bands but usually killed adult male captives without mercy. The whites demonstrated an even more sweeping, persistent, and lethal denial of the humanity of their enemies. They routinely violated treaties, murdered prisoners, poisoned, executed, and tormented even women and children. Scalp hunters and slavers continually provoked Apache revenge by perpetrating outrages—poisoning friendly bands, tossing live babies into fires, and murdering without compunction. Moreover, the Americans never accepted the possibility that the Apache were human beings with an ancient culture deserving of respect. Most whites in the Southwest thought extermination was the best policy, but even white advocates for the Apache thought they should be destroyed culturally and turned into farmers, Christians, and individual landowners.

"The surest way to kill a race is to kill its religion and its ideals," Mescalero Frederick Peso told historian Eve Ball in *Indeh*. "Can anybody doubt that the white race deliberately attempted to do that? This is to kill the soul of a people. And when the spirit is killed, what remains?"

Of course, economics, bureaucracy, greed, racism, and individual actions drove all of the Indian wars. Almost none of the Native American peoples managed to hold onto any significant portion of their original territory, except a few groups like the Hopi whose home territory was so austere and remote that the Americans never bothered to drive them from it. Greed, economics, and racism ensured conflict—but the Apache culture, the terrain of the Southwest, and the role of charismatic war leaders account for the remarkable Apache success in their centuries-long war against the Spanish, the Mexicans, and finally the Americans. The Apache culture fully embraced war and raiding so that the warriors were trained from childhood as perhaps the finest guerrilla warriors in history. The Apache learned to live off the land, seize supplies from their enemies, and avoid reliance on any resources that could be easily seized and destroyed—like the buffalo herds of the Lakota, the sheep herds of the Navajo, or the irrigated crops of the Tohono O'odham. This allowed the Apache to take full advantage of the rugged, difficult terrain of the Southwest, using their knowledge of the land and its resources to outrun and outlast their enemies. The emergence of brilliant, charismatic leaders like Mangas Coloradas, Cochise, Victorio, and Geronimo enabled small groups of warriors to triumph repeatedly against much more numerous and well-supplied foes and to keep their followers fighting even after all reasonable hope of victory had faded.

In the end, the conflict took a terrible toll on the humanity of both sides. The treatment of the Apache remains one of history's indictments of America. "There is no more disgraceful page in the history of our relations with the American Indians than that which conceals the treachery visited upon the Chiricahuas who remained faithful in their allegiance to our people," wrote Bourke, at the conclusion to *On the Border with Crook*.

Geronimo, haunted by dreams that seemed to foreshadow the destruction of his people, observed: "We are vanishing from the earth, yet I cannot think we are useless or Ussen would not have created us . . . For each tribe of men Ussen created, He also made a home. In the land created for any particular tribe He placed whatever would be best for the welfare of that tribe . . . Thus it was in the beginning: The Apaches and their homes each created for the other by Ussen himself. When they are taken from these homes they sicken and die. How long will it be until it is said there are no Apaches?" But Geronimo was also haunted by the memories of what he had done in defense of his people, and the terrible losses on both sides.

> Often I would steal up to the homes of the white settlers and kill the parents. In my hatred, I would even take the little ones out of their cradles and toss them in the air. They would like this and would gurgle with glee, but when they came down I would catch them on my sharp hunting knife and kill them. Now, I wake up groaning and very sad at night when I remember the helpless little children . . . The sun rises and shines for a while and then it goes down, sinking out of sight and it is lost. So it will be with the Indians.

NOTES

p. 142   "There is no more disgraceful . . ." Bourke. *On the Border with Crook*, p. 485.

p. 143   "We are vanishing . . ." Miller, p. 286.

p. 143   "Often I would steal . . ." Roberts, p. 313.

SELECTED
FURTHER
READING LIST
▲

PRIMARY SOURCES

Ball, Eve. *Indeh, An Apache Odyssey*. Provo, UT: Brigham Young University Press, Second printing 1982. Fascinating account of the Apache wars told by leading Chiricahua who were children or apprentice warriors at the time of the conflict. Historian Eve Ball lived on the Mescalero reservation and won the trust of her informants, providing the first full elaboration of the Apache point of view.

———. *In the Days of Victorio*. Tucson: University of Arizona Press, 1970. This tells the story of Nana, Victorio, Kaytennae, and the other Warm Springs or Chihenne leaders. Historian Eve Ball interviewed James Kaywaykla and others who were youngsters in the hunted bands. Essential reading for anyone seeking to understand the Apache Wars.

Betzinez, Jason. *I Fought with Geronimo*. Lincoln: University of Nebraska Press edition of the 1959 original. This memoir of a relative of Geronimo's who took reluctantly to the warpath provides a fascinating glimpse of the divisions among the Apache in confronting the Americans. Betzinez was in Loco's band and was forced off the reservation by the Chiricahua, who he frequently criticizes.

Bourke, John. *On the Border with Crook*. New York, NY: Charles Scribner's Sons, 1891. Time-Life Book reprint. Classics of the

Old West series. This is a wonderful, firsthand account of most of the key events in the Tonto Basin and Chiricahua campaign, together with a stint in the Sioux wars. Bourke became a noted source for historians and anthropologists.

Bourke, John. *An Apache Campaign in the Sierra Madres*. Lincoln: University of Nebraska Press, 1987. Reprint of the 1886 Charles Scribner's Sons edition. A slender, compelling account of General Crook's expedition into the Sierra Madre, which resulted in the surrender of most of the Chiricahua.

Cremony, John. *Life Among the Apaches*. Lincoln: University of Nebraska Press reprint of A. Roman & Company 1868 edition. First Bison Book printing 1983. This is a wonderful, although unreliable, first-person account of the earliest stages of the Apache wars penned by a journalist turned soldier and scout. Cremony's account is by turns thrilling, arrogant, sympathetic, insightful, and racist. He sometimes scrambles his facts but remains a crucial primary source for those events.

Cruse, Thomas. *Apache Days and After*. Lincoln: University of Nebraska Press. Reprint of 1941 Caxton Printers, Ltd. Edition. First Bison Book printing 1987. This is a readable, literate autobiography of Cruse, who won the Congressional Medal of Honor for action against the Apaches. It provides a lot of flavor and detail, although it was written long after the events in question.

Davis, Britton. *The Truth About Geronimo*. Lincoln: University of Nebraska Press reprint of 1929 Yale University Press edition. Tenth Bison Book Printing (1987 first printing). This first-person account of key events in the campaign against the Chiricahua Apache makes fascinating reading, and Davis is an engaging character. The account has shaped subsequent histories and appears surprisingly accurate, although it was written more than 30 years after the events described.

Howard. O. O. *Famous Indian Chiefs I Have Known*. Lincoln: University of Nebraska Press reprint of 1908 Century Company edition. First Bison Book printing 1989. Major General O. O. Howard wrote this somewhat oversimplified but fascinating account of his encounters with some of the most famous Native American leaders, either as a peace negotiator or their enemy in the field. The chapters include meetings with Cochise, Geronimo, Manuelito, Red Cloud, Sitting Bull, Eskiminzin, and others.

HISTORIES

Debo, Angie. *Geronimo, the Man, His Time, His Place*. Norman: University of Oklahoma Press, 1976. The definitive biography of Geronimo, which attempts to present both his triumphs and his failings. The image of Geronimo created by historians changes constantly, from demonization to romantization, but Debo provides the baseline account.

Lockwood, Frank. *The Apache Indians*. Lincoln: University of Nebraska Press, 1938. First Bison Book printing 1987. Lockwood's overview of the Apache wars was the first serious effort. The writing style is steadfast, although a little flat. He also didn't have the wealth of materials from the Apache side that animated later histories.

Melody, Michael E. *The Apache*. New York, NY: Chelsea House, 1989. A young adult book on the Apache.

Roberts, David. *Once They Moved Like the Wind*. New York, NY: Touchstone Books. Simon and Schuster, 1993. The best overall account of the struggle of the Chiricahua Indians, including Geronimo and Cochise. Very readable history integrates both military and Apache accounts.

Sweeney, Edwin. *Cochise*. Norman: University of Oklahoma Press, 1991. The definitive biography of Cochise, and one of the few detailed accounts of the early stages of the Apache wars. Sweeney provides enormous detail, helping break down some of the myths in which Hollywood has shrouded Cochise. Nonetheless, the writing is ponderous compared to *Once They Moved Like the Wind*.

Thrapp, Dan. *Conquest of Apacheria*. Norman: University of Oklahoma Press, 1967. This was one of the first good synthesis of the Apache wars. However, Thrapp sometimes gets bogged down in military detail and doesn't do full justice to the Apache point of view.

————. *Victorio and the Mimbres Apaches*. Norman: University of Oklahoma Press, 1974. Thrapp provides a solid, detailed account of Victorio's struggle to retain his homeland.

Worcester, Donald. *The Apaches: Eagles of the Southwest*. Norman: University of Oklahoma Press, 1992 paperback edition of 1979 original. One of the best overall accounts of the Apache wars, starting with the Spanish and concluding with the imprisonment of the Chiricahua. Worcester produces a comprehensive and solid, although not very flashy, history.

NOVELS

Carter, Forrest. *Watch for Me on the Mountain*. New York, NY: Bantam Doubleday Dell Publishing, 1978. This lyrical little novel is told from Geronimo's point of view. A good read.

Comfort, Will. *Apache*. New York, NY: Dutton & Co., 1931. Bison Book printing now in the 10th edition. This is a well-written book from the point of view of Mangas Coloradas. It skips over historical detail but does a masterful job of trying to capture the Apache point of view.

INDEX

▲

Italic page numbers indicate illustrations.
The letter *m* following a page number indicates a map.